GRADE 1

Morning Jumpstarts: MATH

100 Independent Practice Pages to Build Essential Skills

Marcia Miller & Martin Lee

New York • Toronto • London • Auckland • Sydney
Mexico City • New Delhi • Hong Kong • Buenos Aires

Cover design by Michelle H. Kim
Cover photo © Ronnachai Palas/Shutterstock, Inc.
Interior design by Melinda Belter
Interior illustrations by Teresa Anderko, Melinda Belter, Maxie Chambliss,
Kate Flanagan, Rusty Fletcher, and Sydney Wright; © 2013 by Scholastic Inc.
ISBN: 978-0-545-46414-7
Copyright © 2013 by Scholastic Inc.
Published by Scholastic Inc. All rights reserved.
Printed in the U.S.A.
First printing, January 2013.
4 5 6 7 8 9 10   40   21 20 19 18 17 16

Contents

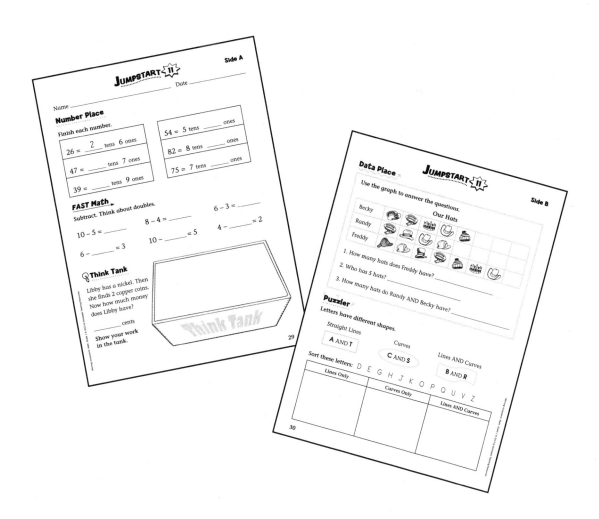

Introduction

In your busy classroom, you know how vital it is to energize children for the tasks of the day. That's why *Morning Jumpstarts: Math, Grade 1* is the perfect tool for you.

The activities in this book provide brief and focused individual practice on grade-level skills children are expected to master. Each Jumpstart is a two-page collection of five activities designed to review and reinforce a range of math skills and concepts children will build throughout the year. The consistent format helps children work independently and with confidence. Each Jumpstart includes these features:

- Number Place
- Fast Math
- Think Tank
- Data Place
- Puzzler

You can use a Jumpstart in its entirety or, because each feature is self-contained, assign sections at different times of the day or to different groups of learners. The Jumpstart activities will familiarize children with the kinds of challenges they will encounter on standardized tests, and provide a review of skills they need to master. (See page 6 for a close-up look at the features in each Jumpstart.)

The Common Core State Standards (CCSS) for Mathematics serve as the backbone of the activities in this book. On pages 7–8, you'll find a correlation chart that details how the 50 Jumpstarts dovetail with the widely accepted set of guidelines for preparing children to succeed in math.

Generally, we have kept in mind the eight CCSS "mathematical practices" that should inform solid math exploration, calculation, and interpretation, even for the youngest learners.

Mathematical Practices

1. Make sense of problems and persevere in solving them.
2. Reason abstractly and quantitatively.
3. Construct viable arguments and critique the reasoning of others.
4. Model with mathematics.
5. Use appropriate tools strategically.
6. Attend to precision.
7. Look for and make use of structure.
8. Look for and express regularity in repeated reasoning.

Morning Jumpstarts: Math, Grade 1 © 2013 by Scholastic Teaching Resources

How to Use This Book

Morning Jumpstarts: Math, Grade 1 can be used in many ways—and not just in the morning! You know the children in your class best, so feel free to pick and choose among the activities, and incorporate those as you see fit. You can make double-sided copies, or print one side at a time and staple the pages together.

We suggest the following times to present Jumpstarts:

- At the start of the school day, as a way to help children settle into the day's routines.
- Before lunch, as children ready themselves for their midday break.
- After lunch, as a calming transition into the afternoon's plans.
- Toward the end of the day, before children gather their belongings to go home, or as homework.

In general, the Jumpstarts progress in difficulty level and build on skills covered in previous sheets. Preview each one before you assign it, to ensure that children have the skills needed to complete them. Keep in mind, however, that you may opt for some children to skip sections, as appropriate, or complete them together at a later time as part of a small-group or whole-class lesson.

Undoubtedly, children will complete their Jumpstart activity pages at different rates. We suggest that you set up a "what to do when I'm done" plan to give children who need more time a chance to finish without interruption. For example, you might encourage children to complete another Jumpstart. They might also choose to read silently, journal, or engage in other kinds of writing.

An answer key begins on page 109. You might want to review answers with the whole class. This approach provides opportunities for discussion, comparison, extension, reinforcement, and correlation to other skills and lessons in your current plans. Your observations can direct the kinds of review or reinforcement you may want to add to your lessons. Alternatively, you may find that having children discuss activity solutions and strategies in small groups is another effective approach.

When you introduce the first Jumpstart, walk through its sections with your class to provide an overview before you assign it and to make sure children understand the directions. Help children see that the activities in each section focus on different kinds of skills, and let them know that the same sections will repeat throughout each Jumpstart, always in the same order and position. You might want to work through the first few Jumpstarts as a group until children are comfortable with the routine and ready to work independently.

You know best how to assign the work to the children in your class. You might, for instance, stretch a Jumpstart over two days, assigning Side A on the first day and Side B on the second. Although the activities on different Jumpstarts vary in difficulty and in time needed, we anticipate that once children are familiar with the routine, most will be able to complete both sides of a Jumpstart in anywhere from 10 to 20 minutes.

A Look Inside

Each two-page Jumpstart includes the following skill-building features.

Number Place The first feature on Side A reviews grade-appropriate place-value skills related to whole numbers, counting, and groupings in tens and ones. Regardless of the particular presentation, children will use their knowledge of place value and their number sense to complete this feature. A solid place-value foundation is essential for success with computation and estimation, and for an overall grasp of numerical patterns and relationships.

Fast Math The second Side A feature addresses necessary grade-level computation skills with the goal of building automaticity, fluency, and accuracy. To work through these exercises, children draw upon their understanding of computation strategies and mathematical properties. In some instances, children will review skills that have been covered previously. This is a good way to keep math skills sharp and to point out to you where revisiting a skill or algorithm may be beneficial.

Think Tank This feature rounds out Side A by offering an original word problem that draws from a wide spectrum of grade-appropriate skills, strategies, and approaches. Some are single-step problems; others require multiple steps to solve. The think tank itself provides a place where children can draw, do computations, and work out their thinking. This is a particularly good section to discuss together, to share solutions, as well as to compare and contrast approaches and strategies. Encourage children to recognize that many problems can be solved in more than one way, or may have more than one solution.

Data Place Every Side B begins with an activity in which children solve problems based on reading, collecting, representing, and interpreting data that is presented in many formats: lists, tables, charts, pictures, and, mostly, in a variety of graphs. In our modern, rapidly changing world, it is essential that children build visual literacy by becoming familiar with many kinds of graphic presentations. This feature presents the kinds of graphs children are likely to encounter online, on TV, and in newspapers and magazines. Many include data from other curriculum areas.

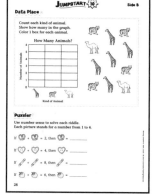

Puzzler Side B always ends with some form of an entertaining challenge: a brainteaser, puzzle, non-routine problem, code, or other engaging task designed to stretch the mind. While some children may find this section particularly challenging, others will relish teasing out trick solutions. This feature provides another chance for group work or discussion. It may prove useful to invite pairs of children to tackle these together. And, when appropriate, invite children to create their own challenges, using ideas sparked by these exercises. Feel free to create your own variations of any brainteasers your class enjoys.

Morning Jumpstarts: Math, Grade 1 © 2013 by Scholastic Teaching Resources

Connections to the Common Core State Standards

As shown in the chart below and on page 8, the activities in this book will help you meet your specific state math standards as well as those outlined in the CCSS. These materials address the following standards for children in grade 1. For details on these standards, visit the CCSS Web site: **www.corestandards.org/the-standards/**.

JS	Operations & Algebraic Thinking								Number & Operations in Base Ten						Measurement & Data				Geometry		
	1.OA.1	1.OA.2	1.OA.3	1.OA.4	1.OA.5	1.OA.6	1.OA.7	1.OA.8	1.NBT.1	1.NBT.2	1.NBT.3	1.NBT.4	1.NBT.5	1.NBT.6	1.MD.1	1.MD.2	1.MD.3	1.MD.4	1.G.1	1.G.2	1.G.3
1									•						•			•	•		
2					•	•	•	•	•						•			•	•		
3	•				•	•	•	•	•									•			
4	•				•	•	•	•	•						•			•			
5	•	•	•		•	•	•	•	•						•			•			
6	•		•		•	•		•		•								•	•		
7	•		•		•	•		•		•								•			
8	•		•	•	•	•	•	•		•					•			•	•	•	
9	•		•	•	•	•	•	•		•					•			•			
10	•		•	•	•	•		•		•								•			
11	•		•	•	•	•	•	•		•								•	•		
12	•		•	•	•	•	•	•		•								•	•		•
13	•		•	•	•	•	•	•	•	•								•			
14	•		•	•	•	•	•	•		•								•	•		
15	•		•	•	•	•	•			•								•	•		•
16	•	•	•	•	•	•	•	•	•	•								•			
17	•	•	•	•	•	•	•	•	•									•	•		
18		•	•	•	•	•	•	•	•	•								•	•		
19	•		•	•	•	•	•	•	•	•								•			
20	•		•	•	•	•	•			•					•	•	•	•			
21	•	•	•	•	•	•	•	•		•	•							•			
22	•		•	•	•	•	•	•	•	•								•			
23	•		•	•	•	•	•	•	•			•					•	•			
24	•	•	•	•		•		•										•	•		
25	•	•	•	•	•	•	•	•	•	•								•			

JS	1.OA.1	1.OA.2	1.OA.3	1.OA.4	1.OA.5	1.OA.6	1.OA.7	1.OA.8	1.NBT.1	1.NBT.2	1.NBT.3	1.NBT.4	1.NBT.5	1.NBT.6	1.MD.1	1.MD.2	1.MD.3	1.MD.4	1.G.1	1.G.2	1.G.3
			Operations & Algebraic Thinking								Number & Operations in Base Ten						Measurement & Data		Geometry		
26	•		•	•	•	•	•	•	•	•	•				•	•		•			
27	•	•	•	•	•	•	•	•				•	•					•	•		
28	•	•	•	•	•	•	•	•	•	•		•	•					•	•		
29	•	•	•	•	•	•	•	•	•	•		•	•					•	•		
30	•	•	•	•	•	•	•	•	•			•		•				•	•		
31	•		•	•	•				•	•	•						•	•			
32	•	•	•	•	•				•	•							•	•			
33		•	•	•	•				•	•		•		•			•	•	•		
34	•	•	•	•	•					•							•	•			
35	•		•	•	•	•	•	•		•					•	•		•			
36	•		•	•		•	•	•		•		•						•			
37	•	•	•	•	•	•	•	•			•	•		•			•	•			
38			•	•		•	•		•	•				•				•			
39	•	•	•		•	•				•	•	•						•			
40	•		•	•	•	•	•	•		•	•	•		•				•	•	•	•
41	•	•	•	•	•	•	•	•		•	•	•		•				•	•	•	
42	•		•	•	•	•	•		•	•	•	•	•	•				•			
43	•		•	•	•	•		•		•	•	•		•			•	•			•
44	•		•	•	•	•	•	•		•	•	•		•				•	•	•	
45	•		•	•	•	•	•	•	•	•	•	•			•	•		•			
46	•	•	•	•	•	•	•	•	•	•			•	•				•			
47			•	•	•	•			•	•	•	•		•				•			•
48	•	•	•	•	•	•	•		•	•	•	•		•				•			
49			•	•	•		•		•	•		•		•	•	•		•	•	•	•
50	•		•	•	•				•	•	•	•		•				•			•

Morning Jumpstarts: Math, Grade 1 © 2013 by Scholastic Teaching Resources

Name _____ Date _____

Number Place

Write how many.

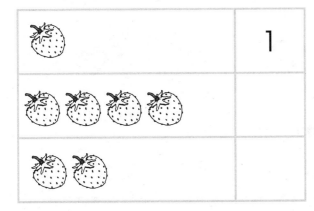

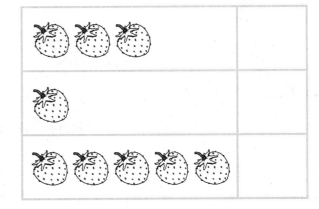

FAST Math ▸

This is a piece of chalk.	⬭
Draw a LONGER piece.	
Draw a SHORTER piece.	

💡 Think Tank

Write your name **inside** the tank.
Write HI **outside**
the tank.
Draw ● on the
side of the tank.

Morning Jumpstarts: Math, Grade 1 © 2013 by Scholastic Teaching Resources

Data Place

Count ☆.

Count ♡.

Count ☾.

Write how many.

How Many?

☆ Star	♡ Heart	☾ Moon
_____	_____	_____

Which is the most? Circle the number.

Puzzler

Connect the dots.

       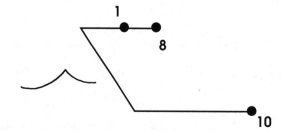

Morning Jumpstarts: Math, Grade 1 © 2013 by Scholastic Teaching Resources

Name _____ Date _____

Number Place

Write how many.

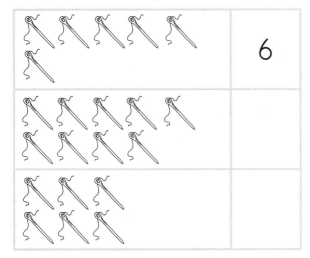

| | 6 |

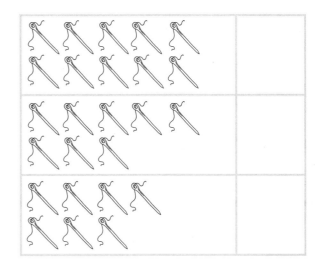

FAST Math ➤

Add.

4 + 1 = _____   2 + 3 = _____   1 + 3 = _____

2 + 1 = _____   4 + 2 = _____   3 + 2 = _____

💡 Think Tank

Write the number that is:

under the bowl. _____

in the bowl. _____

over the bowl. _____

next to the bowl. _____

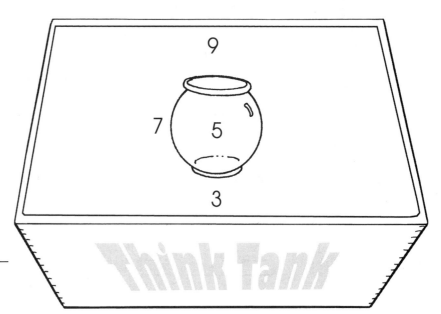

Data Place

Count .

Count .

Count .

Write how many.

How Many?

Apple	_____
Banana	_____
Cherry	_____

1. Which has the fewest?
   Circle the picture in the chart.

2. I see 6 _____ .

Puzzler

X the different one in each row.

Morning Jumpstarts: Math, Grade 1 © 2013 by Scholastic Teaching Resources

Name _____ Date _____

Number Place

Write the missing numbers.

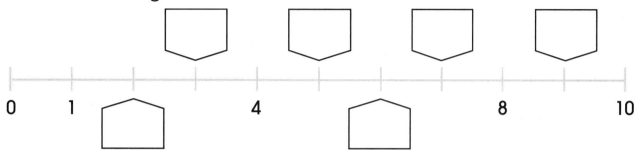

FAST Math

Add.

4 + 3 = _____   5 + 3 = _____   3 + 6 = _____

2 + 5 = _____   4 + 6 = _____   7 + 2 = _____

Think Tank

Hank has these balls.
He has 1 less bat.
How many bats does
Hank have?

In the tank, draw
the bats Hank has.

Write the number.

_____

Morning Jumpstarts, Math: Grade 1 © 2013 by Scholastic Teaching Resources

Data Place

Count 🥄 .

Count 🍴 .

Count 🥤 .

Write how many.

1. I count _____ cups.

2. I count _____ forks.

3. I count _____ spoons.

4. One more spoon would make _____ spoons in all.

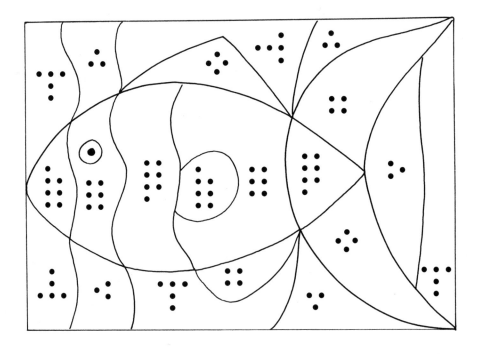

Puzzler

Count and color.
Use the key.

Key	
Number of dots	Color the shape
3	green
4	red
5	blue
6	yellow
7	orange

Morning Jumpstarts: Math, Grade 1 © 2013 by Scholastic Teaching Resources

Name _____ Date _____

Number Place

Draw lines to match words and numbers.

one •	• 4		six •	• 8
two •	• 1		seven •	• 10
three •	• 5		eight •	• 7
four •	• 2		nine •	• 6
five •	• 3		ten •	• 9

FAST Math ➡

Add doubles.

$$\begin{array}{ccccc} 1 & 2 & 3 & 4 & 5 \\ +\ 1 & +\ 2 & +\ 3 & +\ 4 & +\ 5 \\ \hline \\ \underline{\hspace{1cm}} & \underline{\hspace{1cm}} & \underline{\hspace{1cm}} & \underline{\hspace{1cm}} & \underline{\hspace{1cm}} \end{array}$$

💡 Think Tank

Ann is first in line. Zack is sixth in line. How many kids are between Ann and Zack?

There are _____ kids in between.

Show your work in the tank.

Morning Jumpstarts: Math, Grade 1 © 2013 by Scholastic Teaching Resources

Data Place

Count the cubes in each train.

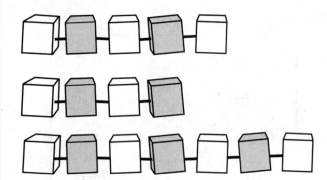

1. How many cubes in the top train? _____

2. How many cubes in the middle train? _____

3. How many cubes in the bottom train? _____

4. Which train is shortest? _____

Puzzler

Add or subtract.
Use the key.

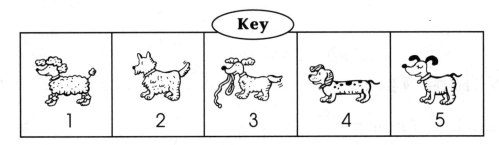

1. + = _____   4. – = _____

2. + = _____   5. – = _____

3. + = _____   6. – = _____

16

Name _____ Date _____

Number Place

Follow the directions.

1. Color the **third** jar red.

2. Color the **ninth** jar blue.

3. Color the **sixth** jar green.

4. ✓ the **second** jar.

5. X the **eighth** jar.

6. Write F on the **fourth** jar.

7. Write S on the **seventh** jar.

8. Write 1 on the **first** jar.

9. Write 10 on the **tenth** jar.

10. The _____ jar is empty.

FAST Math ▶

Add.

$1 + 3 + 2 =$ _____

$5 + 2 + 1 =$ _____

$2 + 4 + 1 =$ _____

$3 + 2 + 4 =$ _____

💡 Think Tank

Rico had cards numbered 1 to 10. He left them outside, and they blew away. He found the 5, 1, 8, 3, and 6 cards. Which number cards got lost?

_____

Show your work in the tank.

Think Tank

Morning Jumpstarts: Math, Grade 1 © 2013 by Scholastic Teaching Resources

Data Place

Count the cubes in each tower.
Write the number on the line.

1. Circle the TALLEST.

2. **X** the SHORTEST.

3. How many cubes

   in the other tower? _____

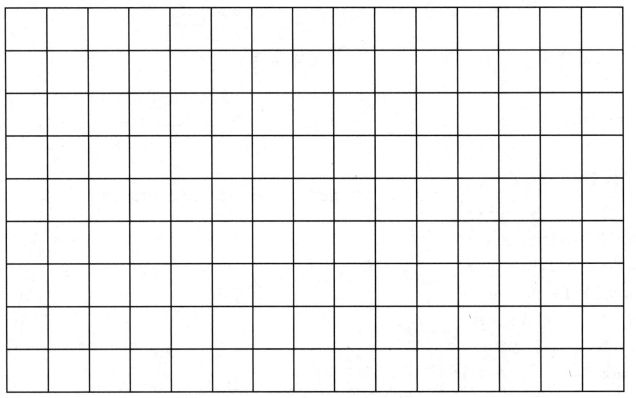

____   ____   ____

Puzzler

Color boxes to draw a picture.

What did you draw? _____

Name _____ Date _____

Number Place

Write how many.

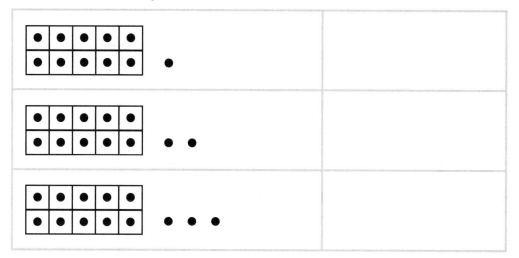

FAST Math

Circle all sums of 6.

6 + 1	3 + 3	1 + 5
2 + 4	4 + 3	4 + 2

Circle all sums of 7.

5 + 2	3 + 4	3 + 5
4 + 4	2 + 5	1 + 6

💡 Think Tank

I am more than 10.
I am less than 18.
You say me when
you count by 5s.
What number am I?

_____

Show your work
in the tank.

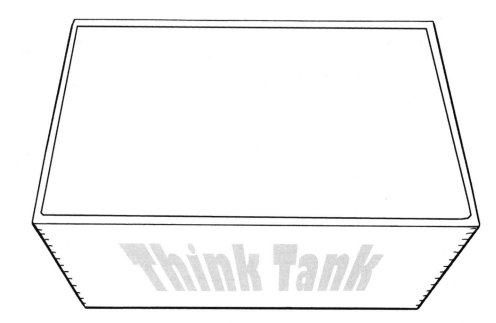

Data Place

How many? Make a table about you.

I have:

Number	Body Part
	Elbows
	Knees
	Mouth
	Thumbs
	Toes
More Than 10	
More Than 100	

Puzzler

Answer the questions about the picture.

How many dots **on** the L? _____

How many dots **inside** the L? _____

How many dots **outside** the L? _____

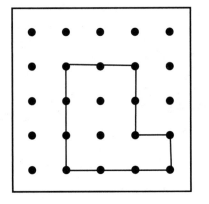

Name _____ Date _____

Number Place

Write how many.

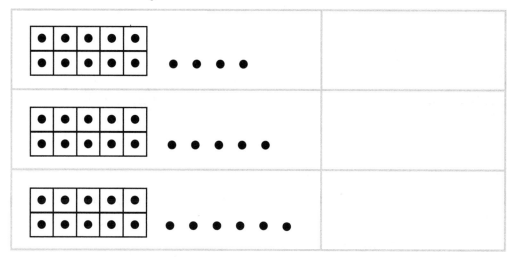

FAST Math →

Circle all sums of 8.

6 + 2	3 + 4	1 + 7
4 + 4	5 + 3	7 + 2

Circle all sums of 9.

7 + 2	3 + 6	3 + 5
4 + 4	5 + 4	8 + 1

💡 Think Tank

Blaze and Star are horses. They need shoes for each hoof. How many horseshoes do they need in all?

_____ horseshoes

Show your work in the tank.

Data Place

Use the graph to answer the questions.

Keys We Have

Rosa						
Kyle						
Isaac						

1. How many children have keys? _____

2. Who has the most keys? _____

3. How many keys does Isaac have? _____

Puzzler

What bird has the biggest eyes?

Use the clues below to answer the question.

_____ _____ _____ _____ _____ _____ _____

The third letter is t.   The fourth letter is r.

The seventh letter is h.   The first letter is o.

The fifth letter is i.   The sixth letters is c.

The second letter is s.

Morning Jumpstarts: Math, Grade 1 © 2013 by Scholastic Teaching Resources

Name _____ Date _____

Number Place

Write how many.

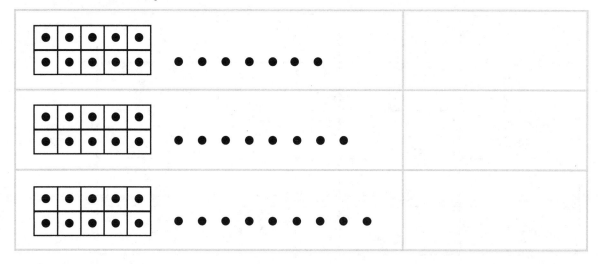

FAST Math

Write each missing addend.

$$\boxed{} \atop {+\ 4 \over 10}$$ $$\boxed{} \atop {+\ 7 \over 10}$$ $$\boxed{} \atop {+\ 2 \over 10}$$ $$\boxed{} \atop {+\ 3 \over 10}$$ $$\boxed{} \atop {+\ 6 \over 10}$$

💡 Think Tank

Greg has 7 books. He did not read 1 of them. How many books did he read?

He read _____ books.

Show your work in the tank.

Data Place

Use the graph to answer the questions.

Seashells We Found

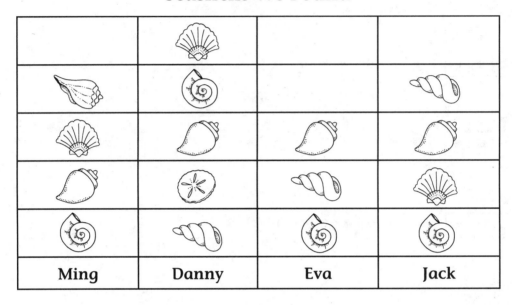

1. How many children found shells? _____

2. Who found the fewest shells? _____

3. Two children found 4 shells each. Write their names.

_____ and _____

Puzzler

Find each shape sum.
Use the numbers in the shapes.

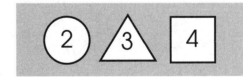

1. ⬦ = _____

2. ▭ = _____

3. ▢◯▢ = _____

4. Draw a shape sum for 7 below.

Morning Jumpstarts: Math, Grade 1 © 2013 by Scholastic Teaching Resources

Name _____ Date _____

Number Place

Draw lines to make matches.

1 ten 0 ones •	• 13
1 ten 1 one •	• 14
1 ten 2 ones •	• 11
1 ten 3 ones •	• 12
1 ten 4 ones •	• 10

1 ten 5 ones •	• 18
1 ten 6 ones •	• 15
1 ten 7 ones •	• 19
1 ten 8 ones •	• 16
1 ten 9 ones •	• 17

FAST Math

Subtract.

$6 - 1 =$ _____ $5 - 2 =$ _____ $4 - 3 =$ _____

$5 - 3 =$ _____ $4 - 2 =$ _____ $6 - 2 =$ _____

Think Tank

Kim is shorter than Rob.
Max is taller than Rob.
Max is taller than Kim.
Draw and label the
boys from tallest
to shortest.

**Show your work
in the tank.**

Data Place

Use the calendar to answer the questions.

Bikes in the Bike Rack

Monday	Tuesday	Wednesday	Thursday	Friday
0	4	9	5	7

1. When were there no bikes in the rack? _____

2. How many bikes were in the rack on Friday? _____

3. Which day had 1 less bike than Thursday? _____

Puzzler

Roll a number cube. Write the number in a box.
Repeat to fill each **+** or **−** problem. Then solve.

1. ☐ + ☐ = ☐   4. ☐ − ☐ = ☐

2. ☐ + ☐ = ☐   5. ☐ − ☐ = ☐

3. ☐ + ☐ = ☐   6. ☐ − ☐ = ☐

Name _____   Date _____

Number Place

Finish the pattern.

3 tens = 30	7 tens =
4 tens =	8 tens =
5 tens =	9 tens =
6 tens =	10 tens =

FAST Math

Subtract.

9 – 7 = _____   8 – 2 = _____   7 – 3 = _____

8 – 5 = _____   7 – 4 = _____   9 – 6 = _____

💡 Think Tank

Zina buys an ice pop for 1 dollar. She buys a puppet for 3 dollars. How much money does she spend?

_____ dollars

Show your work in the tank.

Morning Jumpstarts, Math: Grade 1 © 2013 by Scholastic Teaching Resources

Data Place

Count each kind of animal.
Show how many in the graph.
Color 1 box for each animal.

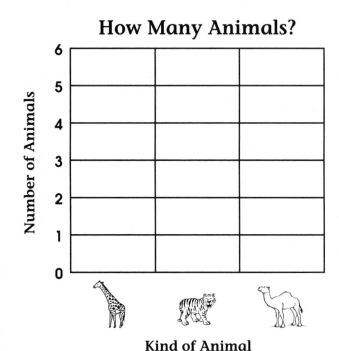

How Many Animals?

Puzzler

Use number sense to solve each riddle.
Each picture stands for a number from 1 to 4.

If ⬤ + ⬤ = 2, then ⬤ = _____

If ♡ + ♡ = 4, then ♡ = _____

If ✏ + ✏ = 8, then ✏ = _____

If 🍓 + 🍓 = 6, then 🍓 = _____

28

Name _____ Date _____

Number Place

Finish each number.

26 = __2__ tens 6 ones	54 = 5 tens _____ ones
47 = _____ tens 7 ones	82 = 8 tens _____ ones
39 = _____ tens 9 ones	75 = 7 tens _____ ones

FAST Math

Subtract. Think about doubles.

$10 - 5 =$ _____ $8 - 4 =$ _____ $6 - 3 =$ _____

$6 -$ _____ $= 3$ $10 -$ _____ $= 5$ $4 -$ _____ $= 2$

💡 Think Tank

Libby has a nickel. Then she finds 2 copper coins. Now how much money does Libby have?

_____ cents

Show your work in the tank.

Data Place

Use the graph to answer the questions.

Our Hats

Becky							
Randy							
Freddy							

1. How many hats does Freddy have? _____

2. Who has 5 hats? _____

3. How many hats do Randy AND Becky have? _____

Puzzler

Letters have different shapes.

Straight Lines   Curves   Lines AND Curves

A AND T   C AND S   B AND R

Sort these letters: D E G H J K O P Q U V Z

Lines Only	Curves Only	Lines AND Curves

Name _____ Date _____

Number Place

Write the number.

6 tens 3 ones = 63	
5 tens 8 ones =	
9 tens 4 ones =	

7 tens 1 one =	
4 tens 9 ones =	
2 tens 6 ones =	

FAST Math

Add or subtract.

$$
\begin{array}{c}
4 \\
+\ 5 \\
\hline
\end{array}
\qquad
\begin{array}{c}
8 \\
-\ 5 \\
\hline
\end{array}
\qquad
\begin{array}{c}
3 \\
+\ 6 \\
\hline
\end{array}
\qquad
\begin{array}{c}
9 \\
-\ 4 \\
\hline
\end{array}
\qquad
\begin{array}{c}
7 \\
-\ 6 \\
\hline
\end{array}
$$

_____   _____   _____   _____   _____

💡 Think Tank

Draw a shape that has 3 sides. Make 2 sides the same length. Write the name of the shape.

_____

Show your work in the tank.

Data Place

Use the chart to answer the questions.

Toy		How much?
Bell		5¢
Frisbee		10¢
Ball		7¢
Yo-Yo		3¢

1. You buy 2 bells. How much do you spend? _____

2. Which 2 different toys cost the same as a Frisbee? _____

   and _____

3. You spend 8¢ on 2 toys. What do you buy? _____

Puzzler

Each row has a different pattern. Draw what comes next.

Morning Jumpstarts: Math, Grade 1 © 2013 by Scholastic Teaching Resources

Name _____ Date _____

Number Place

Write each number.

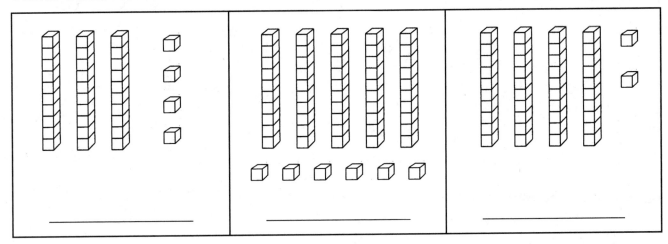

_____   _____   _____

FAST Math ➤

Add.

$4 + 9 =$ _____ $5 + 7 =$ _____ $8 + 3 =$ _____

$6 + 8 =$ _____ $7 + 6 =$ _____ $3 + 9 =$ _____

💡 Think Tank

Edgar has 8 stickers.
He gives some to Ana.
Then Edgar has 5 stickers.
How many did Ana get?

Ana got _____ stickers.

Show your work in the tank.

Data Place

Twelve friends cut out pictures of the fruits they like best.

Use the grid to answer the questions.

1. How many friends cut out fruits? _____

2. How many different kinds of fruits did they pick? _____

3. Which fruit got picked the most? _____

Puzzler

Connect the dots in order. Start at 1.

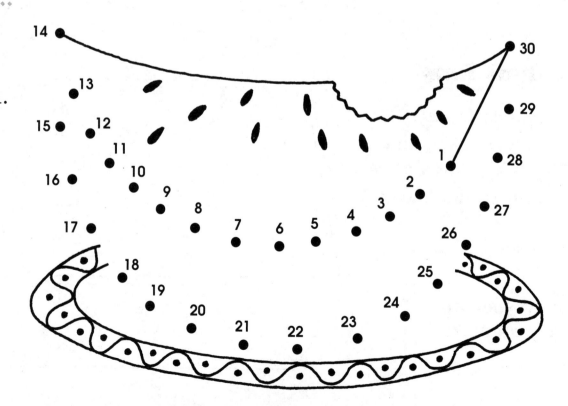

Morning Jumpstarts: Math, Grade 1 © 2013 by Scholastic Teaching Resources

_____ Date _____

Tens	Ones
9	1

Tens	Ones
7	3

Tens	Ones
6	8

_____ _____ _____

FAST Math

Add.

7 + 9 = _____   9 + 8 = _____   8 + 7 = _____

6 + 9 = _____   8 + 8 = _____   9 + 9 = _____

Think Tank

Van has 10¢.
He buys a pin for 6¢.
How much money
does he still have?
Van still has

_____ ¢.

Show your work
in the tank.

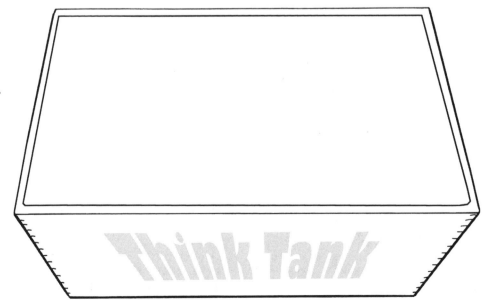

Data Place

Count and graph the shapes. Color 1 box for each shape.

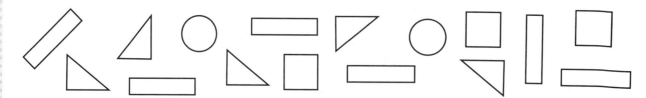

Different Shapes

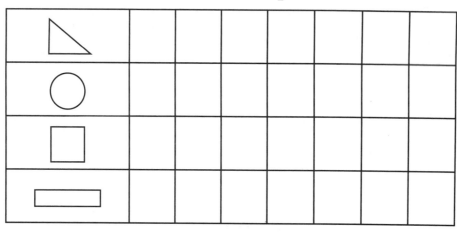

Number of Shapes

1. How many circles? _____

2. How many more triangles than squares? _____

3. How many shapes in all? _____

Puzzler

X the number in each set that does not belong.

40	77	16	15	27
56	55	61	45	19
30	33	69	75	36
70	12	64	51	45

Name _____ Date _____

Number Place

Write how many tens and ones.

53 = _____ tens _____ ones   70 = _____ tens _____ ones

68 = _____ tens _____ ones   25 = _____ tens _____ ones

49 = _____ tens _____ ones   31 = _____ tens _____ ones

FAST Math ➤

Add doubles.

$$\begin{array}{r} 6 \\ +\ 6 \\ \hline \end{array} \qquad \begin{array}{r} 9 \\ +\ 9 \\ \hline \end{array} \qquad \begin{array}{r} 7 \\ +\ 7 \\ \hline \end{array} \qquad \begin{array}{r} 8 \\ +\ 8 \\ \hline \end{array} \qquad \begin{array}{r} 5 \\ +\ 5 \\ \hline \end{array}$$

_____   _____   _____   _____   _____

💡 Think Tank

A garden snake is
11 inches long.
A milk snake is
4 inches shorter.
Draw the snakes.
How long is the
milk snake?

_____ inches

Show your work
in the tank.

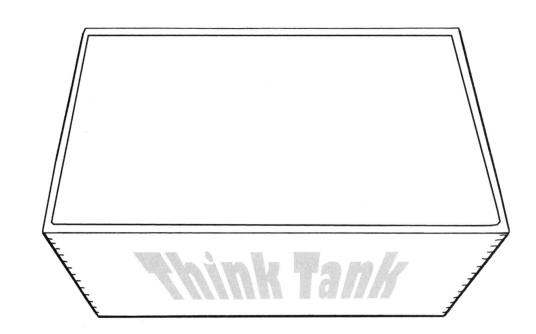

Morning Jumpstarts: Math, Grade 1 © 2013 by Scholastic Teaching Resources

Data Place

Tally the pennies, nickels, and dimes.

How Many?

Coin	Tallies
 (penny)	
(nickel)	
(dime)	

Tally Marks			
1	I	6	⦀⦀ I
2	II	7	⦀⦀ II
3	III	8	⦀⦀ III
4	IIII	9	⦀⦀ IIII
5	⦀⦀	10	⦀⦀ ⦀⦀

How many coins in all?

_____

Puzzler

Color the shapes. Use the key.

Key	
Shape	**Color**
☐	yellow
○	orange
△	red
▭	blue

38

Morning Jumpstarts: Math, Grade 1 © 2013 by Scholastic Teaching Resources

Name _____ Date _____

Number Place

Write the missing numbers.

1		3		5		7		9	
11		13		15		17		19	
21		23		25		27		29	
31		33		35		37		39	

FAST Math ➤

Add.

$7 + 3 + 6 =$ _____

$2 + 5 + 8 =$ _____

$5 + 9 + 4 =$ _____

$7 + 6 + 5 =$ _____

💡 Think Tank

Carly found 11 nests.
Rob found 8 nests.
Who found fewer?

_____

How many fewer?

_____

Show your work
in the tank.

Morning Jumpstarts, Math: Grade 1 © 2013 by Scholastic Teaching Resources

Data Place

Clark collects clocks.
Some have numbers AND hands.
Some have numbers ONLY.

Count and tally each kind.

How Many?

Clocks with:	Tallies
Numbers AND Hands	
Numbers ONLY	

How many more clocks have

numbers ONLY? _____

Puzzler

Look for sums of 10.
Use only 2 boxes for each sum.
Circle every sum you find.
One is done for you.

Hints:

• Find 6 more sums that go
  up and down ↕ .

• Find 6 sums that go across ↔ .

3	4	8	2	1
7	6	2	4	9
2	5	5	7	3
8	1	9	2	6
1	9	3	7	4

Morning Jumpstarts: Math, Grade 1 © 2013 by Scholastic Teaching Resources

Name _____ Date _____

Number Place

Count ON from each number.

36			

48			

29			

57			

FAST Math

Subtract.

$$14 - 5 = \underline{\quad}$$ $$13 - 8 = \underline{\quad}$$ $$11 - 6 = \underline{\quad}$$ $$12 - 4 = \underline{\quad}$$ $$13 - 7 = \underline{\quad}$$

Think Tank

Kay is 9 years old. Finn is 4 years younger than Kay. Dirk is 2 years older than Finn. How old is Dirk?

_____ years old

Show your work in the tank.

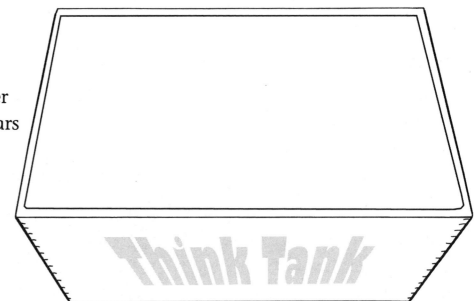

Data Place

Use the table to answer the questions.

Pet Food Sold on Monday

Pet	(bird)	(cat)	(dog)	(fish)
Bags Sold	5	17	20	7

1. How many bags of bird food were sold? _____

2. Which pet owners got 20 bags of food? _____

3. How much more cat food sold than fish food? _____

Puzzler

Trace the shapes. Use the key.

Key	
Shape	**Color**
(oval)	orange
(triangle)	green
(circle)	yellow
(square)	brown
(rectangle)	blue
(hexagon)	red

JUMPSTART 18

Side A

Name ______________________ Date ______________

Number Place

Count BACK from each number.

			99

			87

			73

			61

FAST Math

Subtract.

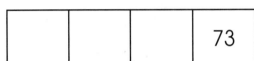

$$\begin{array}{r} 18 \\ -\ 9 \\ \hline \end{array} \qquad \begin{array}{r} 15 \\ -\ 8 \\ \hline \end{array} \qquad \begin{array}{r} 17 \\ -\ 9 \\ \hline \end{array} \qquad \begin{array}{r} 16 \\ -\ 7 \\ \hline \end{array} \qquad \begin{array}{r} 15 \\ -\ 7 \\ \hline \end{array}$$

Think Tank

Draw the next 3 in each pattern.

□ ● □ ● □ ● □ ____ ____ ____

E = A + E = A + ____ ____ ____

(0) (1) (0) (2) (0) (3) (0) ____ ____ ____

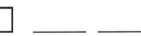

Data Place

Use the Venn diagram to answer the questions.

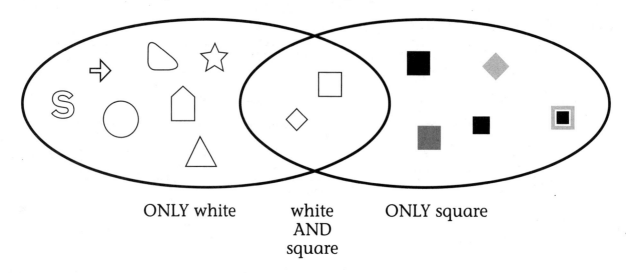

ONLY white   white   ONLY square
                      AND
                      square

Count the shapes in the diagram. How many are:

1. ONLY white? _____

2. ONLY square? _____

3. white AND square? _____

Puzzler

Most numbers on a phone
match letters.
Find the value of each word.
Add the numbers to get the sum.

EXAMPLE
HAY   4 + 2 + 9 = 15

FOX _____

WIN _____

LAW _____

VET _____

BUG _____

Morning Jumpstarts: Math, Grade 1 © 2013 by Scholastic Teaching Resources

Name _____ Date _____

Number Place

Count. Circle groups of 10. Write how many.

✿ ✿	☼ ☼
_____ tens _____ ones	_____ tens _____ ones

FAST Math ▸

Subtract. Think about doubles.

$14 - 7 =$ _____ $18 - 9 =$ _____ $12 - 6 =$ _____

$20 -$ _____ $= 10$ $16 -$ _____ $= 8$ $10 -$ _____ $= 5$

💡 Think Tank

Jalal collects magnets.
He has 8 magnets
of animals. He has
9 magnets of boats.
How many magnets
does Jalal have?
He has

_____ magnets.

Show your work
in the tank.

Data Place

Use the grid to answer the questions.

1. To find ●, start at 0.

   Go **across** _____ and then **up** _____ .

2. To find ▲, start at 0.

   Go **across** _____ and then **up** _____ .

3. To find ■, start at 0.

   Go **across** _____ and then **up** _____ .

4. Go **across** 1 and then **up** 3.

   Draw an **X**.

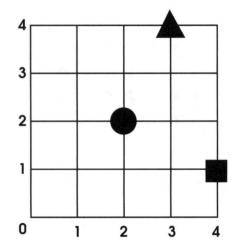

Puzzler

Figure out each pattern.
Write what comes next.

1   2   1   3   1   4   ◯   ◯   ◯

4   14   24   34   44   54   ◯   ◯   ◯

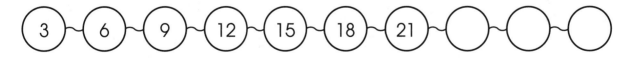

3   6   9   12   15   18   21   ◯   ◯   ◯

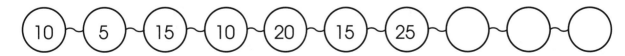

10   5   15   10   20   15   25   ◯   ◯   ◯

Morning Jumpstarts: Math, Grade 1 © 2013 by Scholastic Teaching Resources

Name _____ Date _____

Number Place

X the one in each row that does NOT belong.

33	3 tens 3 ones	3 + 3	thirty-three
65	6 tens 5 ones	60 + 5	sixty-four
87	9 tens 7 ones	90 + 7	ninety-seven
42	2 tens 4 ones	40 + 2	forty-two

FAST Math ▶

Add or subtract.

$$
\begin{array}{cccccc}
15 & 9 & 11 & 8 & 16 & 7 \\
-\ 9 & +\ 8 & -\ 4 & +\ 6 & -\ 7 & +\ 9 \\
\hline
\end{array}
$$

_____ _____ _____ _____ _____ _____

💡 Think Tank

A magic show starts at 1:00. It lasts for 2 hours. What time is it when the show ends?

_____

In the tank, draw a clock to show the time.

Morning Jumpstarts, Math: Grade 1 © 2013 by Scholastic Teaching Resources

Data Place

Use the graph to answer the questions.

Best Things to Collect

Cards	☺ ☺ ☺
Rocks	☺ ☺ ☺ ☺ ☺ ☺
Shells	☺ ☺ ☺ ☺ ☺ ☺ ☺ ☺

Key: ☺ = 1 vote

1. How many people voted for rocks? _____

2. How many people voted for cards? _____

3. Which is the favorite thing to collect? _____

4. How many people picked it? _____

Puzzler

Measure length with the lizard.
Find something for each length.

How Long?	What Is It?
Less Than 1 Lizard	
About 2 Lizards	
About 4 Lizards	
About 6 Lizards	
More Than 7 Lizards	

Morning Jumpstarts: Math, Grade 1 © 2013 by Scholastic Teaching Resources

Name _____   Date _____

Number Place

Circle the value of the underlined digit.

5̲7	**4̲5**	**6̲3**
50 5	50 5	60 6
1̲8	**9̲2̲**	**79̲**
10 1	20 2	90 9

FAST Math ➤

Write **+** or **−** in each cloud.

6 ☁ 3 = 9   12 ☁ 1 = 11   10 ☁ 3 = 7

8 ☁ 3 = 5   11 ☁ 2 = 13   9 ☁ 4 = 13

💡 Think Tank

Ondie buys ribbons.
She gets a red one for 15¢.
She gets a purple one
for 10¢. She gets a
silver one for 25¢.
How much does
Ondie spend in all?

_____ ¢

**Show your work
in the tank.**

Morning Jumpstarts: Math, Grade 1 © 2013 by Scholastic Teaching Resources

Data Place

Use the graph to answer the questions.

Grandpa Goes Fishing

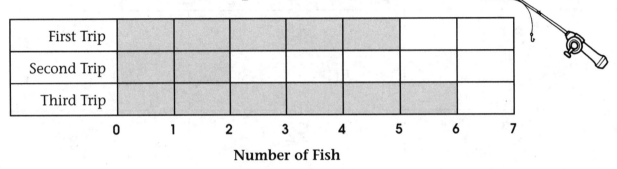

	0	1	2	3	4	5	6	7
First Trip								
Second Trip								
Third Trip								

Number of Fish

1. How many times did Grandpa go fishing? _____

2. When did he catch the most fish? _____

3. When did he catch 5 fish? _____

Puzzler

Sort each number. Write it in the box where it belongs.
Then write your own number that can go in each box.

71   100   6   24   82   33   77   15   28   0   67   54   49   99   12

Numbers < 25	Numbers 26 to 70	Numbers > 70

Morning Jumpstarts: Math, Grade 1 © 2013 by Scholastic Teaching Resources

Name _____ Date _____

Number Place

Write the number that comes just AFTER.

27, _____   48, _____   65, _____

36, _____   50, _____   79, _____

FAST Math ➤

Solve.

If 5 + 7 = 12, then 12 – 5 = _____ .

If 13 – 5 = 8, then 8 + 5 = _____ .

If 9 + 8 = 17, then 17 – 9 = _____ .

If 16 – 7 = 9, then 7 + 9 = _____ .

💡 Think Tank

The teacher serves fruit snacks. She gives bananas to 14 kids. She gives oranges to 9 kids. How many more kids snack on bananas than on oranges?

_____

Show your work in the tank.

Morning Jumpstarts, Math: Grade 1 © 2013 by Scholastic Teaching Resources

Data Place

Use the graph to answer the questions.

At the Bake Sale

Kind of Treat

1. How many kinds of treats were at the bake sale? _____

2. How many and sold?_____

3. Which 2 treats sold the same number? Circle them.

Puzzler

ESTIMATE means to make a smart guess.
Use ordinal numbers to name letters in the word ESTIMATE.

1. What is the fifth letter? _____

2. What is the second letter? _____

3. What is the fourth letter? _____

4. What is the sixth letter? _____

5. What letter is third and seventh?

_____

6. ESTIMATE has 2 of the letter E.
   One E is the first letter. The other E

   is the _____ letter.

52

Name _____ Date _____

Number Place

Write the number that comes just BEFORE.

_____ , 12   _____ , 45   _____ , 66

_____ , 31   _____ , 59   _____ , 80

FAST Math

Write the missing number.

$5 +$ _____ $= 12$ $11 -$ _____ $= 7$ $7 +$ _____ $= 15$

$6 +$ _____ $= 13$ $12 -$ _____ $= 9$ $13 -$ _____ $= 4$

Think Tank

Hakim buys an apple for 20¢. He also buys string cheese for 25¢. How much does he spend on his snack?

He spends _____ ¢.

Show your work in the tank.

Data Place

Write the number pair where you find each building or place.

One is done for you.

1. ___(1, 3)___

2. _____

3. _____

4. _____

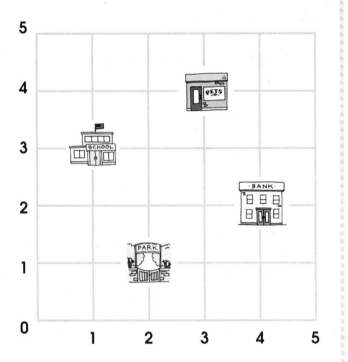

Puzzler

Color the shapes.
Use the key.

Key	
If the number is from	Color the shape
10 to 25	blue
26 to 40	red
41 to 55	yellow
56 to 70	purple
71 to 85	green
86 to 100	orange

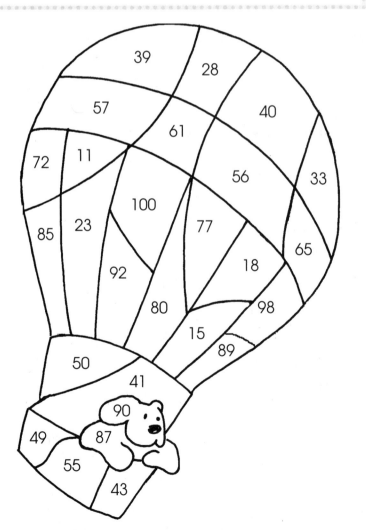

54

Morning Jumpstarts: Math, Grade 1 © 2013 by Scholastic Teaching Resources

Name _____ Date _____

Number Place

Write the number that comes BEFORE and AFTER.

_____ , 17, _____   _____ , 75, _____

_____ , 31, _____   _____ , 60, _____

_____ , 96, _____   _____ , 42, _____

FAST Math ▶

Count.
Write how much.
Circle the greater amount.

_____ ¢

_____ ¢

💡 Think Tank

Nathan buys 3 hot dogs.
They cost $2 each.
How much does he
spend on hot dogs?

$ _____

Show your work
in the tank.

Morning Jumpstarts: Math, Grade 1 © 2013 by Scholastic Teaching Resources

Data Place

Some numbers have lines ONLY.
Some have curves ONLY.
Some have lines AND curves.

0 1 2 3 4 5 6 7 8 9

Write 0 to 9 in the loops where they belong.

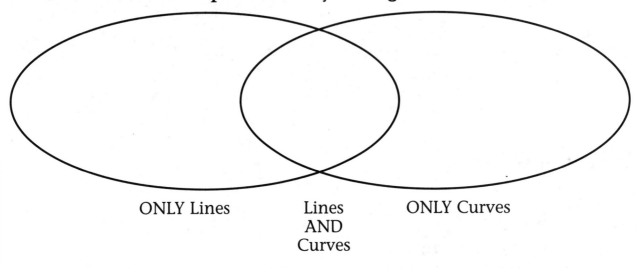

ONLY Lines   Lines AND Curves   ONLY Curves

Puzzler

Three numbers in each balloon can make a number fact.
X the number that does NOT belong.

3   5
9   12

4   5
8   13

14   8
11   6

8   10
15   7

16   9
7   8

56

Name _____ Date _____

Number Place

Write the missing numbers.

27, _____ , _____ , _____ , _____ , 32

48, _____ , _____ , _____ , _____ , 53

76, _____ , _____ , _____ , _____ , 81

FAST Math ➤

Add or subtract. Write ¢.

$$
\begin{array}{cccccc}
10¢ & 7¢ & 9¢ & 15¢ & 16¢ & 9¢ \\
- 2¢ & + 4¢ & + 3¢ & - 5¢ & - 8¢ & + 6¢ \\
\hline
\end{array}
$$

_____ _____ _____ _____ _____ _____

💡 Think Tank

I am a 2-digit number.
I am less than 40.
I name all the fingers,
toes, eyes, and ears
you have.
What number am I?

_____

Show your work
in the tank.

Data Place

The children in Ezra's class drew creepy crawlies. Then they counted their drawings.

Use the table to answer the questions.

Creepy Crawlies	
Slug	5
Snail	11
Worm	8

1. Which creepy crawly did 5 children draw? _____

2. How many snail pictures were there? _____

3. How many more worms than slugs? _____

Puzzler

Pretend that the thick line is a mirror.
Half of the design is ABOVE the mirror.
Shade the other half BELOW the thick line.

Name _____ Date _____

Number Place

Compare. Write **<** or **>**.

68 ◯ 62   74 ◯ 81   92 ◯ 90

45 ◯ 41   89 ◯ 93   52 ◯ 47

FAST Math

Solve. Draw lines to match facts in the same family.

$6 + 7 =$ ☐ •

$9 + 8 =$ ☐ •

$8 + 5 =$ ☐ •

• $13 - 8 =$ ☐

• $13 - 7 =$ ☐

• $17 - 8 =$ ☐

💡 Think Tank

Margo has 10 nickels. She spends 3 of them on gumballs. How many nickels does Margo still have? Margo has

_____ nickels.

It is the same as

_____ cents.

Show your work in the tank.

Morning Jumpstarts: Math, Grade 1 © 2013 by Scholastic Teaching Resources

Data Place

Look at the boxes. Then draw each line. Start at ●.

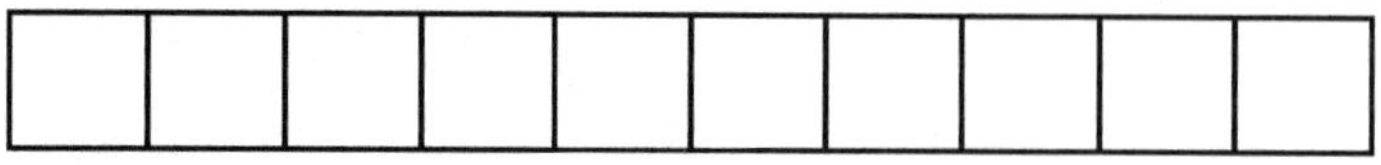

Draw a line about 8 boxes long.

○ ●

Draw a line about 3 boxes long.

○ ●

Draw a line longer than 10 boxes.

○ ●

Order the lines from 1 (longest) to 3 (shortest).
Write the numbers in the circles.

Puzzler

Do a length hunt. Use your shoe as a "ruler."
Find 4 things for each part of the chart. List them.

Shorter than my shoe	About the Same as my shoe	Longer than my shoe

Name _____ Date _____

Number Place

Look at the numbers in the cloud.
Four are ODD. Four are EVEN.
Write the numbers in the chart.

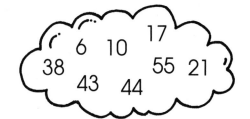

ODD Numbers	EVEN Numbers

FAST Math

Add.

$$36 + 10$$ $$83 + 10$$ $$57 + 10$$ $$64 + 10$$ $$75 + 10$$ $$49 + 10$$

_____ _____ _____ _____ _____ _____

Think Tank

Grammy loves to bake.
She baked 6 cakes, 4 pies,
and 24 muffins. How
many things did she
bake in all? She baked

_____ things.

Show your work
in the tank.

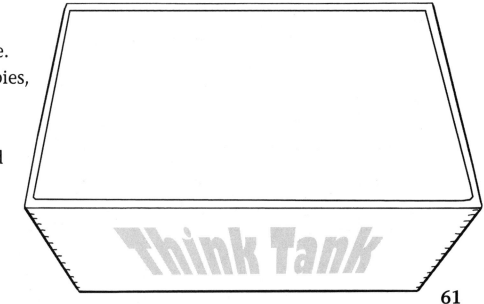

Data Place

Color bars on the graph to show each price.

How Many Pennies?

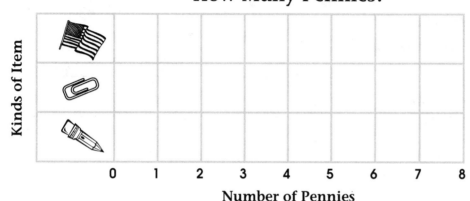

Key

✎ = 5¢

🇺🇸 = 7¢

📎 = 2¢

1. How much more for a than a ? _____

2. How much for 6 📎 ? _____

3. How much for 1 of each item? _____

Puzzler

Each row has a different pattern.
Draw what comes next.

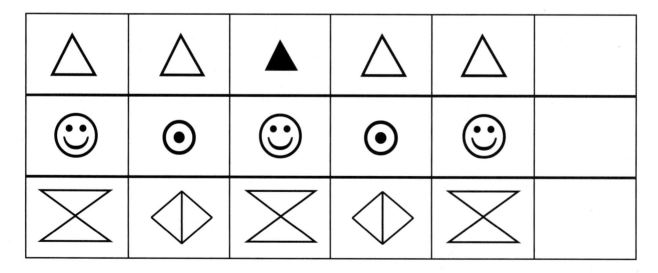

Name _____ Date _____

Number Place

Skip count aloud by 5s. Write each number you say.

5, 10, _____ , _____ , _____ , _____ , _____ ,

40, _____ , _____ , _____ , _____ , _____ ,

_____ , 75, _____ , _____ , _____ , _____ , 100

FAST Math →

Subtract.

45	98	56	61	73	84
− 10	− 10	− 10	− 10	− 10	− 10

_____ _____ _____ _____ _____ _____

💡 Think Tank

Circle the shape in each row that does NOT belong.

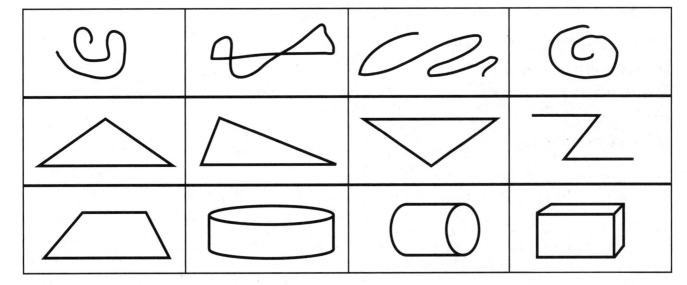

Data Place

Mrs. Lobel took her class to lunch. She saw that 8 kids drank juice, 9 drank milk, and 6 kids drank water.

Show this data in a graph. Make bars with letters. Count from the bottom up.

• Write a **J** for each juice.

• Write an **M** for each milk.

• Write a **W** for each water.

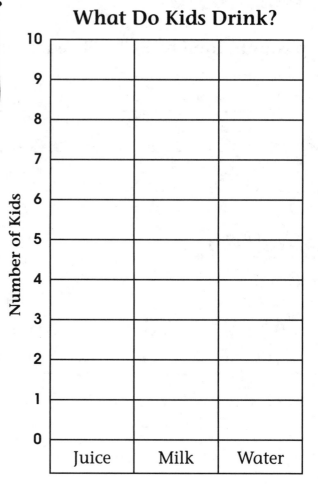

What Do Kids Drink?

Puzzler

Write 1, 3, 7, and 9 ONCE in each empty box. Make each row ↔ and column ↕ have a sum of 15.

64

Name _____ Date _____

Number Place

Skip count aloud by 10s. Write each number you say.

10, _____ , _____ , _____ , _____ ,

_____ , _____ , _____ , _____ , 100

FAST Math ➤

Add.

44	38	51	62	17	29
+ 30	+ 50	+ 40	+ 20	+ 60	+ 70

_____   _____   _____   _____   _____   _____

💡 Think Tank

Each house on Key Road has a number. The first five house numbers are 101, 103, 105, 107, and 109. What is the next house number? The next

number is _____ .

Show your work in the tank.

Data Place

Kids told what they do before bed.

Use the data to make a graph.

Before bed I like to:	Tallies
Play with my pet.	ℍℍ III
Read a book.	ℍℍ ℍℍ
Watch TV.	ℍℍ I

What Kids Do Before Bed

Play with my pet.												
Read a book.												
Watch TV.												

0   2   4   6   8   10   12

Number of Votes

1. How many more kids read than watch TV? _____

2. How many kids play with a pet or watch TV? _____

Puzzler

Write how much each shape costs.

 3¢   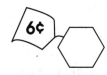 6¢   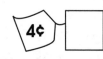 4¢

1.

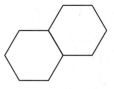

_____

2.

_____

3.

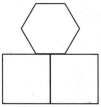

_____

4.

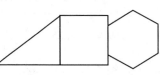

_____

Name _____ Date _____

Number Place

Count BACK aloud by 10s. Write the numbers you say.

100, 90, _____ , _____ , _____ , _____ ,

_____ , _____ , _____ , _____ , 0

FAST Math ▶

Subtract.

85	92	51	64	78	39
− 60	− 70	− 40	− 30	− 50	− 20
_____	_____	_____	_____	_____	_____

💡 Think Tank

The art teacher gets 32 new paintbrushes and 45 new markers. How many new art items is this in all?

_____ new art items

Show your work in the tank.

Data Place

Darla cleaned her room. Look what she found under her bed!

Show the data in a graph. Color 1 box for each item.

Item	Tally
Crayons	~~||||~~	
Socks	|||
Toys	~~||||~~

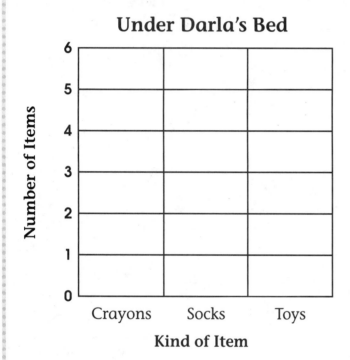

Under Darla's Bed

Number of Items

6
5
4
3
2
1
0

Crayons   Socks   Toys

Kind of Item

How many items did Darla find in all?

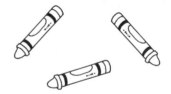

_____

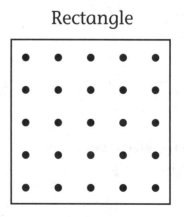

Puzzler

Draw the shapes.
Start and stop each line at a dot.

Triangle

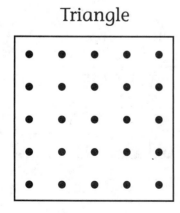

Square

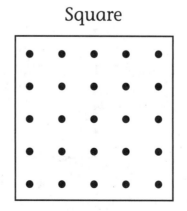

Rectangle

68

Name _____ Date _____

Number Place

Write the number that is 10 MORE.

9 _____   46 _____   54 _____

28 _____   87 _____   65 _____

FAST Math ➜

What time is it?

___ : ___   ___ : ___   ___ : ___   ___ : ___

💡 Think Tank

There are 65 children who go ice skating. Then 12 of them go inside to rest. How many children keep skating?

_____ kids keep skating.

Show your work in the tank.

Data Place

Draw ✓ in the graph for each fruit you see.

How Many Fruits?

Apples	
Bananas	
Cherries	
Pears	

Key: ✓ = 1 piece of fruit

1. How many cherries? _____

2. Two fruits together equal the number of pears.

   They are _____ and _____ .

Puzzler

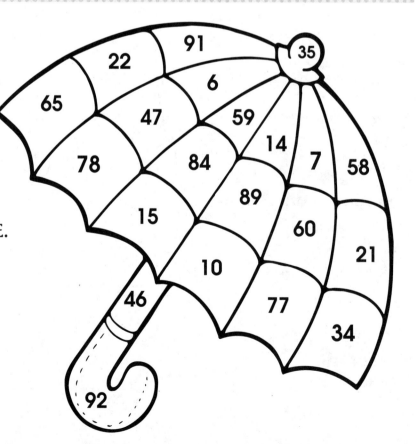

Color ODD numbers RED.

Color EVEN numbers BLUE.

70

Morning Jumpstarts: Math, Grade 1 © 2013 by Scholastic Teaching Resources

Name _____ Date _____

Number Place

Write the number that is 10 LESS.

13 _____   74 _____   98 _____

61 _____   85 _____   72 _____

FAST Math →

Draw hands to show each time.

2:00   6:00   11:00

💡 Think Tank

A zoo has 14 monkeys and 11 parrots. Each gets 1 apple a day. How many apples do all the animals eat in 2 days?

They eat _____ apples in all.

Show your work in the tank.

Morning Jumpstarts, Math: Grade 1 © 2013 by Scholastic Teaching Resources

Data Place

Momo is a circus monkey.
He wears a hat and a vest.

• He has 1 purple hat and 1 red hat.

• He has 1 blue vest and 1 yellow vest.

Color each DIFFERENT outfit Momo can wear.

Puzzler

Connect the dots.
Start at 0.
Count by 10s.

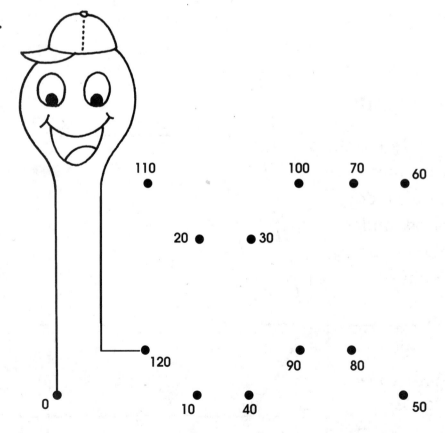

110   100   70   60

20   30

120   90   80

0   10   40   50

Name _____ Date _____

Number Place

Match words and numbers.

twenty •	• 80		ten •	• 90
forty •	• 40		thirty •	• 10
sixty •	• 100		fifty •	• 70
eighty •	• 20		seventy •	• 30
hundred •	• 60		ninety •	• 50

FAST Math

What time is it?

_____ : _____   _____ : _____   _____ : _____   _____ : _____

💡 Think Tank

Tina has 6 coins. They are worth 50¢ in all. What coins does Tina have? Draw and label them.

Show your work in the tank.

Data Place

Use the calendar to answer the questions.

Weather in May

Sunday	Monday	Tuesday	Wednesday	Thursday	Friday	Saturday
1	2	3	4	5	6	7

1. How many days in a week? _____

2. How many days had 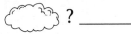 ? _____

3. How many days had ? _____

4. What was the weather on Thursday? _____

5. Which were bad days for picnics? _____

_____

Puzzler

START with the number at the left.
Do what each arrow says. Use the key.
Write each NEW number.
Keep going to the end of the row.

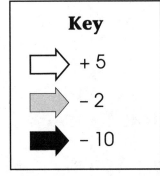

53   ☐ ☐ ☐

86   ☐ ☐ ☐

74

Name _____ Date _____

Number Place

How many dimes?

20 pennies = _____ dimes   30 pennies = _____ dimes

40 pennies = _____ dimes   60 pennies = _____ dimes

80 pennies = _____ dimes   90 pennies = _____ dimes

FAST Math

Draw hands on the clocks to show each time.

10:30   5:30   9:00

💡 Think Tank

Three kids count steps from the door to their seats. Lia takes 15 steps. Pam takes 4 steps less than Lia. Ari takes 6 more steps than Pam. Who is nearest the door?

_____ is nearest.

Show your work in the tank.

Morning Jumpstarts, Math: Grade 1 © 2013 by Scholastic Teaching Resources

Data Place

Plan a perfect day.
On the chart, draw or write what
you would do at each time of day.

Wake up	Morning	Noon	Afternoon	Night

Puzzler

Color squares to make
an animal on this grid.

Color squares to make
a pattern on this grid.

Name _____ Date _____

Number Place

Round to the nearest 10¢.

17¢ → _____ ¢   32¢ → _____ ¢   56¢ → _____ ¢   78¢ → _____ ¢

44¢ → _____ ¢   65¢ → _____ ¢   81¢ → _____ ¢   93¢ → _____ ¢

FAST Math

Add.

$$\begin{array}{r} 24 \\ + \ 32 \\ \hline \end{array} \qquad \begin{array}{r} 63 \\ + \ 14 \\ \hline \end{array} \qquad \begin{array}{r} 48 \\ + \ 51 \\ \hline \end{array} \qquad \begin{array}{r} 56 \\ + \ 23 \\ \hline \end{array} \qquad \begin{array}{r} 32 \\ + \ 45 \\ \hline \end{array} \qquad \begin{array}{r} 70 \\ + \ 17 \\ \hline \end{array}$$

_____   _____   _____   _____   _____   _____

Think Tank

Cody's favorite TV show starts at 7:30. It lasts one half-hour. What time does it say on Cody's clock when the show ends?

Write the time in numbers on the clock.

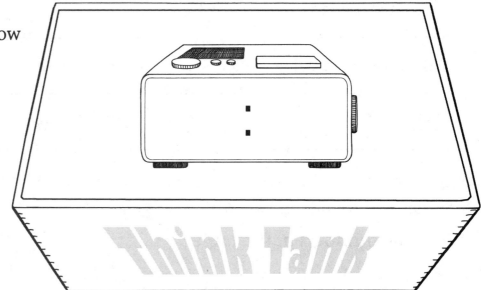

Data Place

Look at the ruler. Then draw each line. Start at ●.

| | 1 | 2 | 3 | 4 | 5 | 6 |

Draw a line about 3 inches long.

◯ ●

Draw a line about 5 inches long.

◯ ●

Draw a line less than 2 inches long.

◯ ●

Order the lines from 1 (longest) to 3 (shortest).
Write the numbers in the circles.

Puzzler

Jin got a new piggy bank. His dad will give him
pennies for it each day. Here is his plan.

Which day?	1	2	3	4	5	6	7
How many pennies?	1	2	4	8	16		

Figure out Dad's pattern. How many
pennies will Jin get on Day 6? On Day 7?

Write the numbers in the table.

Morning Jumpstarts: Math, Grade 1 © 2013 by Scholastic Teaching Resources

Name _____ Date _____

Number Place

Round to the nearest number of dimes.

37¢ → _____ dimes   42¢ → _____ dimes   66¢ → _____ dimes

54¢ → _____ dimes   75¢ → _____ dimes   91¢ → _____ dimes

FAST Math

Round each addend to the nearest 10. Estimate the sum.

47 → ☐   22 → ☐   61 → ☐
+ 31 → ☐   + 59 → ☐   + 17 → ☐
─────────   ─────────   ─────────

about: _____   about: _____   about: _____

💡 Think Tank

Mr. Lim has 28 children in his class. There are 15 boys. How many children are girls? There are

_____ girls.

Show your work in the tank.

Data Place

Three friends counted birds at the lake.

Add or subtract to find the missing numbers.

	Ducks	Swans	Total
Roscoe	16	3	
Noah	17		22
Kerry		6	19

1. Noah saw _____ ducks.

2. _____ saw 6 swans.

3. Roscoe saw _____ birds in all.

4. Who counted the fewest ducks? _____

Puzzler

This is a number puzzle.

• Each row ⟷ needs a 1, 2, 3, and 4.

• Each column ↕ needs a 1, 2, 3, and 4.

• Numbers can be in any order.

Write the missing numbers.

2	1	4	3
4			1
1			4
3	4	1	2

80

Morning Jumpstarts: Math, Grade 1 © 2013 by Scholastic Teaching Resources

Name _____ Date _____

Number Place

Round to the nearest ten.

16 → ____   21 → ____   45 → ____   67 → ____

33 → ____   54 → ____   71 → ____   88 → ____

FAST Math

Round each number to the nearest 10. Estimate the difference.

$$49 \rightarrow \boxed{}$$
$$-\ 31 \rightarrow \boxed{}$$

about: _____

$$72 \rightarrow \boxed{}$$
$$-\ 29 \rightarrow \boxed{}$$

about: _____

$$86 \rightarrow \boxed{}$$
$$-\ 13 \rightarrow \boxed{}$$

about: _____

Think Tank

Finish each day name. Order the days from 1 to 7.
Count Sunday as Day 1. Write the numbers in the boxes.

☐ F r _ _ _ _ _   ☐ T u e _ _ _ _

☐ M o _ _ _ _ _   ☐ T h u r _ _ _ _

☐ S a t _ _ _ _   ☐ W e d n e s _ _ _

☐ S u _ _ _ _

Data Place

Renee has $10. She goes
to the movies.

**Use the price list to answer
the questions.**

PRICES	
Child's Ticket	$5
Large Popcorn	$3
Small Popcorn	$2
Large Soda	$2
Small Soda	$1

1. How much money does Renee have

   after she buys a ticket? _____

2. Her dad told her to bring home $1.

   But Renee wants popcorn and soda.

   What can she order? _____

   _____

3. How much would it cost for 4 children to buy

   movie tickets? _____

Puzzler

Write EVERY 2-digit number you can.
Use the 3 numbers in the boxes ONLY.
Try for all 6 numbers.

| 8 | 2 | 4 |

Circle the greatest number. Underline the least number.

Morning Jumpstarts: Math, Grade 1 © 2013 by Scholastic Teaching Resources

Name _____ Date _____

Number Place

Regroup 10 ones as 1 ten.

3 tens 12 ones = ___4___ tens ___2___ ones

4 tens 15 ones = _____ tens _____ ones

5 tens 19 ones = _____ tens _____ ones

6 tens 17 ones = _____ tens _____ ones

FAST Math ➔

Subtract.

$$
\begin{array}{cccccc}
64 & 78 & 83 & 95 & 52 & 44 \\
-\ 33 & -\ 16 & -\ 71 & -\ 23 & -\ 12 & -\ 21 \\
\hline
\end{array}
$$

💡 Think Tank

Shari made up a number pattern. Write the next 3 numbers.

Show your work in the tank.

98, 87, 76, 65, 54,

_____, _____, _____,

Think Tank

Data Place

Some first graders took out library books.

Graph the data in the table.

Let ☐ stand for 1 book.

Child	Books
Jamila	3
Opal	6
Riley	4

Books Taken Out

Jamila	
Opal	
Riley	
Key: ☐ = 1 book	

Puzzler

Get the rocket to the moon!
Count by 2s from 2 to 50.
Shade the boxes as you go.

53	48	51	43	57		
50	46	49	51	23		
51	45	44	49	15		
43	42	63	65	7	11	93
39	41	40	31	53	13	6	1	3
37	38	35	23	11	8	5	4	**2**
36	26	24	22	21	9	10
34	28	25	20	15	13	12
32	30	23	18	16	14	11

Name _____ Date _____

Number Place

Order the numbers from LEAST to GREATEST.

70, 55, 67 _____

62, 55, 66 _____

94, 49, 50 _____

118, 75, 104 _____

FAST Math

Add. Regroup 10 ones as 1 ten.

33	54	22	55	12	61
+ 37	+ 16	+ 28	+ 35	+ 48	+ 19
___	___	___	___	___	___

Think Tank

Here's a tricky riddle: How many 1s are on a clock face?

Draw a picture in the tank to help you solve the riddle.

Data Place

How many veggies did Vicki pick?

Count and tally them.
Then write the number.

Vicki's Veggies

Veggie	Tally	Number
Carrots		4
Peppers		
Potatoes		

1. Vicki picked the most _____ .

2. Vicki picked 4 _____ .

3. She picked _____ veggies in all.

Puzzler

Each ◇ = 1 dart.

Write the score each dartboard shows.

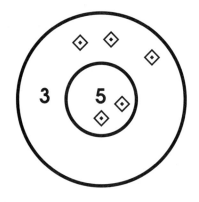

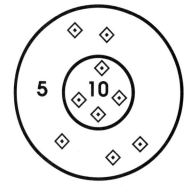

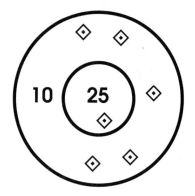

Score: _____   Score: _____   Score: _____

Morning Jumpstarts: Math, Grade 1 © 2013 by Scholastic Teaching Resources

Name _____ Date _____

Number Place

Order the numbers from GREATEST to LEAST.

41, 33, 28 _____

49, 59, 39 _____

83, 33, 38 _____

105, 117, 99 _____

FAST Math ➤

Add. Regroup when needed.

41	24	46	11	26	43
+ 28	+ 26	+ 24	+ 33	+ 51	+ 17
——	——	——	——	——	——

💡 Think Tank

Show half of each square in the tank.

- Draw a RED line to show half one way.

- Draw a BLUE line to show half a different way.

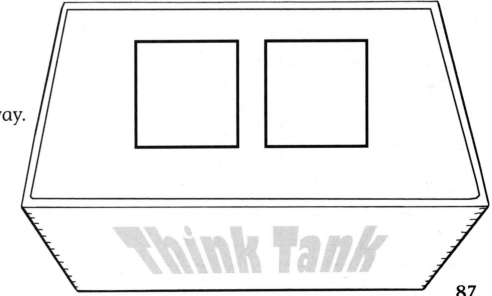

Data Place

Lizzy brushes her hair each day. She counts the brushstrokes:

Monday	60
Tuesday	40
Wednesday	40
Thursday	50
Friday	30

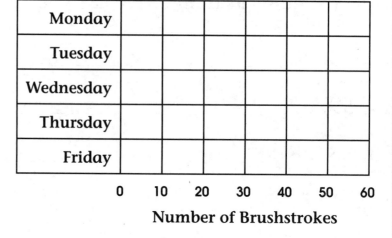

Brushstrokes for Lizzy

Color bars to show Lizzy's brushstrokes each day.

Find the difference between MOST and LEAST strokes. _____

Puzzler

Write **H** for HALVES. Write **F** for FOURTHS.

Name _____ Date _____

Number Place

Write in number form.

thirty-three _____   eighty-six _____

seventy-five _____   forty-one _____

ninety-nine _____   fifteen _____

FAST Math →

Subtract. Regroup 1 ten as 10 ones.

50	80	90	70	40	60
− 18	− 27	− 32	− 36	− 28	− 11

_____ _____ _____ _____ _____ _____

💡 Think Tank

Draw some coins to make 41¢. Use ONLY dimes, nickels, and pennies. Write the value on each coin.

Show your work in the tank.

Morning Jumpstarts: Math, Grade 1 © 2013 by Scholastic Teaching Resources

Data Place

Finish the table. Draw tallies or write numbers.

Books Read Last Week

Books Read	Tally	Number of People
0	II	
1		6
2		9
3	THL	

1. How many people read NO books? _____

2. How many people read 1 book? _____

3. How many books did 9 people read? _____

Puzzler

Use the key to solve the problems.

Key

| 11 | 22 | 60 | 75 | 99 |

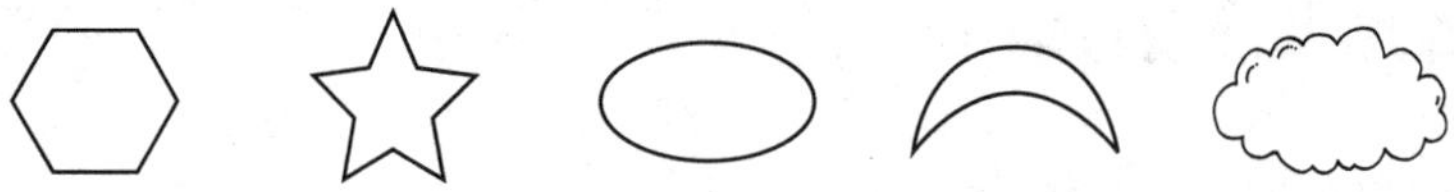

1. 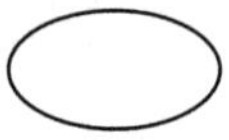 ⬭ + ⬡ = _____

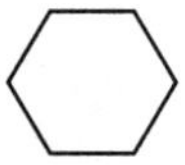

2.  ⌒ + ☆ = _____

3.  ⌒ − ⬭ = _____

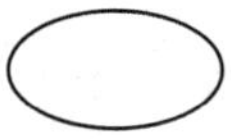

4.  ☁ − ⌒ = _____

Name _____ Date _____

Number Place

Write the number that comes BETWEEN.

38, ____, 40   27, ____, 29   42, ____, 44

63, ____, 65   16, ____, 18   51, ____, 53

45, ____, 47   99, ____, 101   70, ____, 72

FAST Math ➤

Subtract. Regroup when needed.

$$\begin{array}{r} 49 \\ -\ 16 \\ \hline \end{array} \qquad \begin{array}{r} 70 \\ -\ 36 \\ \hline \end{array} \qquad \begin{array}{r} 67 \\ -\ 27 \\ \hline \end{array} \qquad \begin{array}{r} 82 \\ -\ 31 \\ \hline \end{array} \qquad \begin{array}{r} 98 \\ -\ 23 \\ \hline \end{array} \qquad \begin{array}{r} 90 \\ -\ 68 \\ \hline \end{array}$$

💡 Think Tank

Arun is 19 years old. Ree is 13 years old. How many years younger is Ree than Arun?

Ree is _____ years younger.

Show your work in the tank.

Data Place

Kids voted on best things to do at a fair.

Use the chart to answer the questions at right.

What to Do	Votes
Face Painting	15
Spin Art	9
Ring Toss	11
Fun Nails	6

1. What did 11 kids want to do?

   _____

2. What got the most votes?

   _____

3. How many more voted for Spin Art than Fun Nails?

   _____

4. Find the difference between MOST and FEWEST votes.

   _____

Puzzler

Connect the dots.
Start at 120.
Count back by 10s.

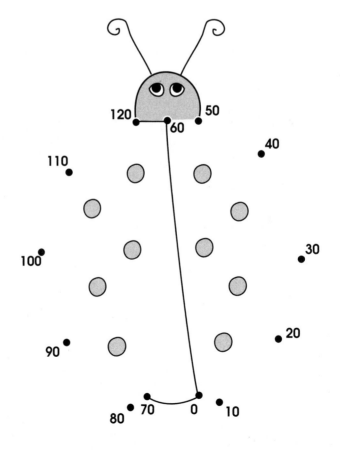

92

Morning Jumpstarts: Math, Grade 1 © 2013 by Scholastic Teaching Resources

Name _____ Date _____

Number Place

Compare. Write **<** or **>**.

68 ◯ 86   37 ◯ 17   24 ◯ 42

75 ◯ 69   98 ◯ 89   88 ◯ 91

FAST Math ➤

Add or subtract. Watch the signs!

55	64	76	41	37	98
− 14	+ 34	− 26	+ 37	+ 52	− 76
_____	_____	_____	_____	_____	_____

💡 Think Tank

1 hour = 60 minutes

How many minutes are in half an hour? Use mental math to solve. Half an hour has

_____ minutes.

Use the tank if you need to.

Morning Jumpstarts: Math, Grade 1 © 2013 by Scholastic Teaching Resources

Data Place

Finish the table.

First Graders at Moss School

Class	Girls	Boys	Total
1A		14	27
1B	14	14	
1C	14		27

1. Which is the biggest class? _____

2. Which class has the fewest girls? _____

3. Finish the sentence: Classes 1A and 1C both have

_____

_____

Puzzler

Write the letter
to make each
number sentence true.

A = 10	E = 20	I = 30	O = 40	U = 50

$24 + \underline{\hspace{1cm}} = 54$ $100 - \underline{\hspace{1cm}} = 60$

$\underline{\hspace{1cm}} - 25 = 25$ $69 + \underline{\hspace{1cm}} = 79$

$\underline{\hspace{1cm}} + 16 = 56$ $48 - 28 = \underline{\hspace{1cm}}$

Morning Jumpstarts: Math, Grade 1 © 2013 by Scholastic Teaching Resources

Name _____   Date _____

Number Place

Sort the numbers. Write them where they belong.

86	8	63	95	39	48	12	31
	0	77	26	81	17	89	40

Less Than 20	Between 21 and 50	Greater Than 50

FAST Math ▶

Add or subtract. Watch the signs!

```
  67        25        76        49        56        87
- 36      + 35      + 13      - 28      + 34      - 57
_____    _____    _____    _____    _____    _____
```

💡 Think Tank

A hammer is 9 inches long. An ax is 18 inches long. How much longer is the ax? Draw a picture to compare them. The ax is

_____ inches longer.

Show your work in the tank.

Think Tank

Morning Jumpstarts: Math, Grade 1 © 2013 by Scholastic Teaching Resources

Data Place

Ann   Ben   Fritz   Dawn   Ella   Carl   Gina   Henry

Sort the children by what they are wearing.
Write their names where they belong in the Venn diagram.

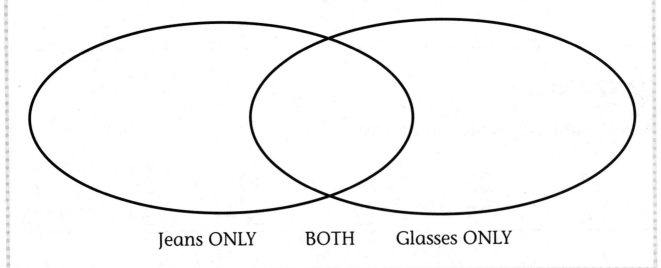

Jeans ONLY   BOTH   Glasses ONLY

Puzzler

Count the blocks in each figure.
Count ALL the blocks, even hidden ones.

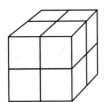 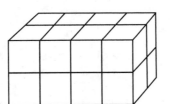 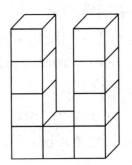

_____   _____   _____

Morning Jumpstarts: Math, Grade 1 © 2013 by Scholastic Teaching Resources

Name _____ Date _____

Number Place

Write how many tens and ones.

72 = _____ tens _____ ones   90 = _____ tens _____ ones

89 = _____ tens _____ ones   63 = _____ tens _____ ones

24 = _____ tens _____ ones   31 = _____ tens _____ ones

FAST Math

Round to the nearest dime. Estimate the sum.

57¢ → ☐   32¢ → ☐   43¢ → ☐
+ 22¢ → ☐   + 49¢ → ☐   +38¢ → ☐

about: _____ ¢   about: _____ ¢   about: _____ ¢

Think Tank

Rex is a dog. He hid some bones in his yard. Rex hid more than 5 bones, but fewer than 8 bones. Rex did NOT hide 6 bones. How many bones did Rex hide? Rex hid

_____ bones.

Show your work in the tank.

Morning Jumpstarts: Math, Grade 1 © 2013 by Scholastic Teaching Resources

97

Data Place

These are the longest names in Amy's class.

Varastadt Bagdazarian — called Vara
Annabella Giangregorio — called Anna
Shakuntala Satapathy — called Tala

Fill in the table about the names.

Child	Letters in First Name	Letters in Last Name	Total Number of Letters
Vara			
Anna			
Tala			

1. Who has the longest first name? _____

2. Who has the longest last name? _____

3. Who has the longest full name? _____

Puzzler

Look at the 2 lines.
Which is longer?
Use a ruler to know for sure.

What did you find out? _____

_____

Morning Jumpstarts: Math, Grade 1 © 2013 by Scholastic Teaching Resources

Name _____ Date _____

Number Place

Write the number that is 10 MORE.

64 _____   35 _____   71 _____

57 _____   88 _____   46 _____

Write the number that is 10 LESS.

35 _____   92 _____   67 _____

14 _____   43 _____   58 _____

FAST Math

Round to the nearest dime. Estimate the difference.

58¢ → ☐   82¢ → ☐   93¢ → ☐
− 31¢ → ☐   − 49¢ → ☐   − 57¢ → ☐

about: _____ ¢   about: _____ ¢   about: _____ ¢

Think Tank

A field mouse ate 4 wild onions, 5 grapes, and 6 acorns. How many pieces of food did the mouse eat?

_____ pieces of food

Show your work in the tank.

Data Place

Best at the Playground

Jungle Gym	 👍 👍 👍 👍 👍
Swing	 👍 👍 👍 👍
Seesaw	 👍 👍 👍 👍 👍 👍 👍

Key: 👍 = 1 vote

Use the graph to answer the questions.

1. Five people voted for _____ .

2. Which playground place got the most votes? _____

3. Which got the fewest votes? _____

4. How many children voted? _____

Puzzler

Pretend to pick up both objects.
Circle the one that weighs more.

1.  or

2.  or

3.  or

4.  or

Morning Jumpstarts: Math, Grade 1 © 2013 by Scholastic Teaching Resources

Name _____ Date _____

Number Place

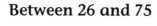

Write 4 different numbers in each cloud.

Less Than 25   Between 26 and 75   Greater Than 76

FAST Math ➤

X the equations that are FALSE.

$4 + 7 = 47$	$12 - 6 = 18$	$8 + 8 = 16$
$7 + 8 = 15$	$40 + 60 = 100$	$20 - 10 = 30$

💡 Think Tank

Mario made a round pizza. Draw lines to show how to cut his pizza into FOURTHS. How do you know how many pieces to make?

Show your work in the tank.

Data Place

Tally and write the number for every letter in this tongue twister.

Ted fed Fred bread.

Letter	Tally	Number
a		
b		
d		
e		
f		
r		
t		

Puzzler

Pretend to fill both objects.
Circle the one that holds more.

1.    or

2.  or

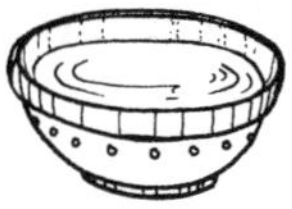

3.  or

4.  or

102

Morning Jumpstarts: Math, Grade 1 © 2013 by Scholastic Teaching Resources

Name _____ Date _____

Number Place

Write the missing numbers.

77, _____ , _____ , _____ , _____ , 82

49, _____ , _____ , _____ , _____ , 54

98, _____ , _____ , _____ , _____ , 103

FAST Math

Write the missing number to make the equation TRUE.

$\boxed{} - 8 = 6$	$\boxed{} + 10 = 20$	$18 - \boxed{} = 10$
$20 + \boxed{} = 30$	$15 = \boxed{} + 10$	$20 = \boxed{} - 2$

Think Tank

Write every DIFFERENT addition fact you know that equals 10.

Show your work in the tank.

Data Place

January in Oswego, New York, in 1966 was very snowy. The calendar shows when snow fell.

Use the calendar to answer the questions.

Sunday	Monday	Tuesday	Wednesday	Thursday	Friday	Saturday
25	26	27	28	29	30	31
Snow: 0 inches	Snow: 0 inches	Snow: 8 inches	Snow: 12 inches	Snow: 11 inches	Snow: 21 inches	Snow: 50 inches

1. When did the snow start to fall? _____

2. How many days in a row got snow? _____

3. How much snow fell in all on Wednesday,

   Thursday, and Friday? _____

4. Was this more or less than the amount of snow

   that fell on January 31? _____

Puzzler

Write the second part of each math word.
Use the letter bank to help.

1. e _____

2. hun _____

3. num _____

4. quar _____

5. twen _____

6. ze _____

Letter Bank

ro

ty

ter

ber

qual

dred

Morning Jumpstarts: Math, Grade 1 © 2013 by Scholastic Teaching Resources

Name _____ Date _____

Number Place

Finish the number line.

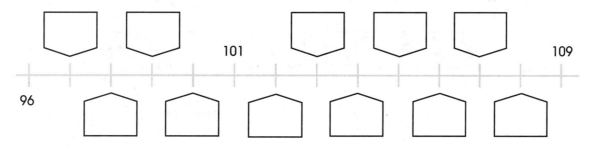

FAST Math

Shade the fractions.

| one half | one half | one fourth | one quarter |

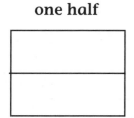
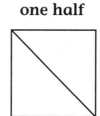

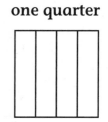

Think Tank

Look at the shape in the first box.
Color the shape where you see it in the row.

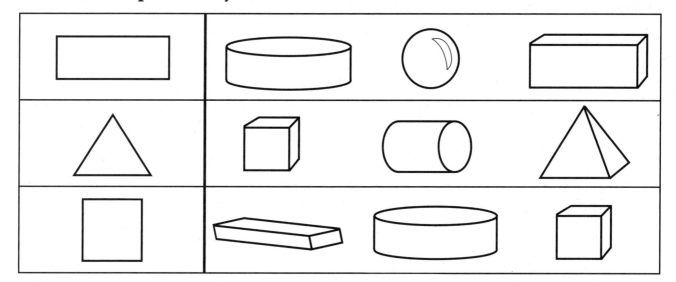

Data Place

Measure the ribbon and pencil.
Use paper clips AND ones cubes.
Write each length to the nearest unit.

_____ paper clips   _____ ones cubes

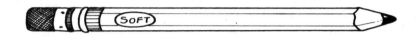

_____ paper clips   _____ ones cubes

Why does each object have 2 DIFFERENT measurements?

_____

_____

_____

Puzzler

Use number sense.
Figure out each missing digit.

$$
\begin{array}{r} 7\ 5 \\ -\ \boxed{}\ 3 \\ \hline 6\ 2 \end{array}
\qquad
\begin{array}{r} \boxed{}\ 3 \\ +\ 3\ 6 \\ \hline 8\ 9 \end{array}
\qquad
\begin{array}{r} \boxed{}\ 9 \\ -\ 1\ 2 \\ \hline 5\ 7 \end{array}
\qquad
\begin{array}{r} 2\ \boxed{} \\ +\ 4\ 1 \\ \hline 7\ 0 \end{array}
$$

Morning Jumpstarts: Math, Grade 1 © 2013 by Scholastic Teaching Resources

Name _____   Date _____

Number Place

Count. Circle tens. Write how many.

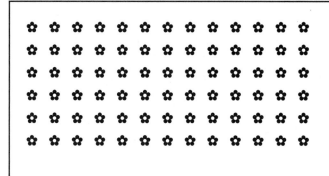

_____ tens _____ ones   _____ tens _____ ones

FAST Math

Circle the fraction for the shaded part.

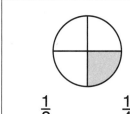   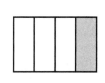

$\frac{1}{2}$ $\frac{1}{4}$ $\frac{1}{2}$ $\frac{1}{4}$ $\frac{1}{2}$ $\frac{1}{4}$ $\frac{1}{2}$ $\frac{1}{4}$

💡 Think Tank

Eli has 22 marbles.
He keeps 12 of them.
He gives the rest to his
2 sisters. Each gets
the same number.
How many marbles
does each sister get?

_____ marbles each

**Show your work
in the tank.**

Data Place

Children at a park took a survey. They voted for a favorite summer treat. The table shows the votes.

Use the table to answer the questions.

Summer Treat	Votes
Ice Cream	117
Lemonade	86
Watermelon	71

1. Eighty-six kids voted for _____.

2. _____ got the most votes.

3. _____ got 71 votes.

4. How many more voted for lemonade than watermelon?

   _____

Puzzler

Write a story problem.
Use any numbers from the box.
Be sure you can find the answer.

4	8	11
13	15	20

_____

_____

_____

_____

Answers

Jumpstart 1
Number Place: (Top to bottom) 4, 2; 3, 1, 5
Fast Math: Check children's pictures.
Think Tank: Check children's pictures.
Data Place: star—3, heart—4, moon—2; circle 4
Puzzler:

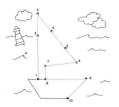

Jumpstart 2
Number Place: (Top to bottom) 9, 6; 10, 8, 7
Fast Math: (Left to right) 5, 5, 4; 3, 6, 5
Think Tank: 3, 5, 9, 7
Data Place: (Top to bottom) 6, 7, 5
1. Circle cherry **2.** apples
Puzzler: 3rd hat, 4th bowl, 2nd ladybug

Jumpstart 3
Number Place: 2, 3, 5, 6, 7, 9
Fast Math: (Left to right) 7, 8, 9; 7, 10, 9
Think Tank: 3 bats; check children's pictures.
Data Place: 1. 6 **2.** 7 **3.** 9 **4.** 10
Puzzler: Check children's coloring.

Jumpstart 4
Number Place: Check children's matches.
Fast Math: 2, 4, 6, 8, 10
Think Tank: 4
Data Place: 1. 5 **2.** 4 **3.** 7 **4.** middle train
Puzzler: 1. 6 **2.** 8 **3.** 7 **4.** 3 **5.** 3 **6.** 1

Jumpstart 5
Number Place: Check children's work; fifth
Fast Math: (Left to right) 6, 7; 8, 9
Think Tank: 2, 4, 7, 9, 10
Data Place: 1. tower of 6 **2.** tower of 3 **3.** 4
Puzzler: Drawings will vary; check children's work.

Jumpstart 6
Number Place: 11, 12, 13
Fast Math: sums of 6—3 + 3, 1 + 5, 2 + 4, 4 + 2; sums of 7—5 + 2, 3 + 4, 2 + 5, 1 + 6
Think Tank: 15
Data Place: 2, 2, 1, 2, 10; answers will vary.
Puzzler: 12, 2, 11

Jumpstart 7
Number Place: 14, 15, 16
Fast Math: sums of 8—6 + 2, 1 + 7, 4 + 4, 5 + 3; sums of 9—7 + 2, 3 + 6, 5 + 4, 8 + 1

Think Tank: 8
Data Place: 1. 3 **2.** Kyle **3.** 4
Puzzler: ostrich

Jumpstart 8
Number Place: 17, 18, 19
Fast Math: 6, 3, 8, 7, 4
Think Tank: 6
Data Place: 1. 4 **2.** Eva **3.** Ming, Jack
Puzzler: 1. 6 **2.** 8 **3.** 10 **4.** Check children's composite shape drawings.

Jumpstart 9
Number Place: Check children's matches.
Fast Math: (Left to right) 5, 3, 1; 2, 2, 4
Think Tank: Max, Rob, Kim
Data Place: 1. Monday **2.** 7 **3.** Tuesday
Puzzler: Answers will vary; check children's work.

Jumpstart 10
Number Place: (Top to bottom) 40, 50, 60; 70, 80, 90, 100
Fast Math: (Left to right) 2, 6, 4; 3, 3, 3
Think Tank: 4
Data Place:

Puzzler: (Top to bottom) 1, 2, 4, 3

Jumpstart 11
Number Place: (Top to bottom) 4, 3; 4, 2, 5
Fast Math: (Left to right) 5, 4, 3; 3, 5, 2
Think Tank: 7
Data Place: 1. 7 **2.** Becky **3.** 9
Puzzler: lines only—E, H, K, V, Z; curves only—O; lines and curves—D, G, J, P, Q, U

Jumpstart 12
Number Place: (Top to bottom) 58, 94; 71, 49, 26
Fast Math: 9, 3, 9, 5, 1
Think Tank: triangle; check children's drawings for isosceles triangles.
Data Place: 1. 10¢ **2.** ball, yo-yo **3.** bell, yo-yo
Puzzler:

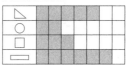

Jumpstart 13
Number Place: 34, 56, 42
Fast Math: (Left to right) 13, 12, 11; 14, 13, 12
Think Tank: 3
Data Place: 1. 12 **2.** 4 **3.** bananas

Puzzler:

Jumpstart 14
Number Place: 91, 73, 68
Fast Math: (Left to right) 16, 17, 15; 15, 16, 18
Think Tank: 4
Data Place:

◁					
○					
□					
▭					

1. 2 **2.** 2 **3.** 16
Puzzler: 56, 12, 16, 51, 19

Jumpstart 15
Number Place: (Top to bottom) 5, 3; 6, 8; 4, 9; 7, 0; 2, 5; 3, 1
Fast Math: 12, 18, 14, 16, 10
Think Tank: Check children's drawings; 7
Data Place:

Coin	Tallies
🪙	卌 III
🪙	卌
🪙	III

16 coins in all

Puzzler: Check children's pictures.

Jumpstart 16
Number Place:

1	3	5	7	9
11	13	15	17	19
21	23	25	27	29
31	33	35	37	39

Fast Math: (Left to right) 16, 15; 18, 18
Think Tank: Rob; 3
Data Place:

Clocks with:	Tallies
Numbers AND Hands	卌 II
Numbers ONLY	卌 卌

3 more clocks have numbers only

Puzzler:

3	4	8	2	1
7	6	2	4	9
2	5	5	7	3
8	1	9	2	6
6	7	3	6	4

Jumpstart 17
Number Place: (Left to right) 37, 38, 39; 49, 50, 51; 30, 31, 32; 58, 59, 60
Fast Math: 9, 5, 5, 8, 6
Think Tank: 7
Data Place: 1. 5 **2.** dog **3.** 10 bags
Puzzler: Check children's coloring.

Answers

Jumpstart 18
Number Place: (Left to right) 96, 97, 98; 84, 85, 86; 70, 71, 72; 58, 59, 60
Fast Math: 9, 7, 8, 9, 8
Think Tank: ● □ ● ; E = A; ④ ⓪ ⑤
Data Place: 1. 7 **2.** 5 **3.** 2
Puzzler: 18, 19, 16, 19, 14

Jumpstart 19
Number Place: 4, 7; 6, 4
Fast Math: (Left to right) 7, 9, 6; 10, 8, 5
Think Tank: 17
Data Place: 1. (2, 2) **2.** (3, 4) **3.** (4, 1)
4. Check children's graphs for X at (1, 3).
Puzzler: 1, 6, 1; 64, 74, 84; 24, 27, 30; 20, 30, 25

Jumpstart 20
Number Place: 3 + 3; sixty-four; 87; 2 tens 4 ones
Fast Math: 6, 17, 7, 14, 9, 16
Think Tank: Check that children draw a clock showing 3:00.
Data Place: 1. 6 **2.** 3 **3.** shells **4.** 8
Puzzler: Check children's answers, which may vary.

Jumpstart 21
Number Place: (Left to right) 50, 5, 60; 10, 2, 9
Fast Math: (Left to right) +, −, −; −, +, +
Think Tank: 50
Data Place: 1. 3 **2.** third trip **3.** first trip
Puzzler: numbers < 25—0, 6, 12, 15, 24; numbers 26 to 70—28, 33, 49, 54, 67; numbers > 70—71, 77, 82, 99, 100

Jumpstart 22
Number Place: (Left to right) 28, 49, 66; 37, 51, 80
Fast Math: 7, 13, 8, 16
Think Tank: 5
Data Place: 1. 5 **2.** 7 **3.** circle cookie and donut
Puzzler: 1. M **2.** S **3.** I **4.** A **5.** T **6.** eighth (or last)

Jumpstart 23
Number Place: (Left to right) 11, 44, 65; 30, 58, 79
Fast Math: (Left to right) 7, 4, 8; 7, 3, 9
Think Tank: 45
Data Place: 2. (2,1) **3.** (4,2) **4.** (3,4)
Puzzler: Check children's coloring.

Jumpstart 24
Number Place: (Left to right) 16, 18; 74, 76; 30, 32; 59, 61; 95, 97; 41, 43
Fast Math: 47, 38; circle 47¢
Think Tank: 6
Data Place: only lines—1, 4, 7; only curves—0, 3, 6, 8; lines and curves—2, 5, 9
Puzzler: (Left to right) 5, 4, 11; 10, 8

Jumpstart 25
Number Place: (Left to right) 28, 29, 30, 31; 49, 50, 51, 52; 77, 78, 79, 80

Fast Math: 8¢, 11¢, 12¢, 10¢, 8¢, 15¢
Think Tank: 24
Data Place: 1. slug **2.** 11 **3.** 3
Puzzler:

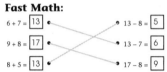

Jumpstart 26
Number Place: (Left to right) >, <, >; >, <, >
Fast Math:

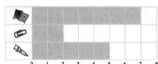

Think Tank: 7, 35
Data Place: Check children's lines; 2, 3, 1
Puzzler: Answers will vary; check for reasonableness.

Jumpstart 27
Number Place: odd—17, 21, 43, 55; even—6, 10, 38, 44
Fast Math: 46, 93, 67, 74, 85, 59
Think Tank: 34
Data Place:

1. 5¢ **2.** 12¢ **3.** 14¢
Puzzler:

Jumpstart 28
Number Place: (Left to right) 15, 20, 25, 30, 35, 45, 50, 55, 60, 65, 70, 80, 85, 90, 95
Fast Math: 35, 88, 46, 51, 63, 74
Think Tank:

Data Place:

	Juice	Milk	Water
9		M	
8	J	M	
7	J	M	
6	J	M	W
5	J	M	W
4	J	M	W
3	J	M	W
2	J	M	W
1	J	M	W

Puzzler:

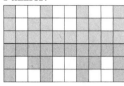

Jumpstart 29
Number Place: (Left to right) 20, 30, 40, 50, 60, 70, 80, 90
Fast Math: 74, 88, 91, 82, 77, 99
Think Tank: 111
Data Place:

Play with my pet.						
Read a book.						
Watch TV.						

1. 4 **2.** 14
Puzzler: 1. 12¢ **2.** 10¢ **3.** 14¢ **4.** 13¢

Jumpstart 30
Number Place: (Left to right) 80, 70, 60, 50, 40, 30, 20, 10
Fast Math: 25, 22, 11, 34, 28, 19
Think Tank: 77
Data Place:

Darla found 14 items in all.

Puzzler: Pictures may vary; check children's drawings.

Jumpstart 31
Number Place: (Left to right) 19, 56, 64; 38, 97, 75
Fast Math: 4:00, 7:00, 10:00, 1:00
Think Tank: 53
Data Place:

Apples	✓ ✓ ✓
Bananas	✓ ✓
Cherries	✓ ✓ ✓ ✓ ✓
Pears	✓ ✓ ✓ ✓ ✓
Key: ✓ = 1 piece of fruit	

1. 6 **2.** apples, bananas
Puzzler:

Jumpstart 32
Number Place: (Left to right) 3, 64, 88; 51, 75, 62
Fast Math: Check children's clock-face drawings.
Think Tank: 50

Morning Jumpstarts: Math, Grade 1 © 2013 by Scholastic Teaching Resources

Data Place: Check children's coloring. Look for 4 outfits: purple hat + blue vest; purple hat + yellow vest; red hat + blue vest; red hat + yellow vest.
Puzzler:

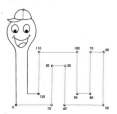

Jumpstart 33
Number Place: Check children's matches.
Fast Math: 12:30, 4:30, 8:30, 2:30
Think Tank: 4 dimes + 2 nickels
Data Place: 1. 7 **2.** 2 **3.** 2 **4.** Sunny **5.** Tuesday, Friday
Puzzler: (Left to right) 43, 48, 46; 84, 74, 79

Jumpstart 34
Number Place: (Left to right) 2, 3; 4, 6; 8, 9
Fast Math: Check children's clock-face drawings.
Think Tank: Pam
Data Place: Answers will vary; check children's charts for reasonableness.
Puzzler: Answers will vary; check children's drawings and patterns.

Jumpstart 35
Number Place: (Left to right) 20, 30, 60, 80; 40, 70, 80, 90
Fast Math: 56, 77, 99, 79, 77, 87
Think Tank: 8:00
Data Place: Check children's lines; 2, 1, 3
Puzzler: 32, 64

Jumpstart 36
Number Place: (Left to right) 4, 4, 7; 5, 8, 9
Fast Math: 50, 30, 80; 20, 60, 80; 60, 20, 80
Think Tank: 13
Data Place:

	Ducks	Swans	Total
Roscoe	16	3	**19**
Noah	17	**5**	22
Kerry	**13**	6	19

1. 17 **2.** Kerry **3.** 19 **4.** Kerry
Puzzler:

2	1	4	3
4	**3**	**2**	1
1	**2**	**3**	4
3	4	1	2

Jumpstart 37
Number Place: (Left to right) 20, 20, 50, 70; 30, 50, 70, 90
Fast Math: 50, 30, 20; 70, 30, 40; 90, 10, 80
Think Tank: (Top to bottom) Friday, Monday, Saturday, Sunday, Tuesday, Thursday, Wednesday; 6, 2, 7, 1, 3, 5, 4
Data Place: 1. $5 **2.** small popcorn + large soda or large popcorn + small soda **3.** $20
Puzzler: 24, 28, 42, 48, 82, 84

Jumpstart 38
Number Place: 5, 5; 6, 9; 7, 7
Fast Math: 31, 62, 12, 72, 40, 23
Think Tank: 43, 32, 21
Data Place:

Jamila	☐☐☐
Opal	☐☐☐☐☐☐
Riley	☐☐☐☐

Key: ☐ = 1 book

Puzzler:

	53	48	51	43	57		
50	46	49	51	23			
	51	45	44	49	15		
	43	42	63	65	7	11	93
39	41	40	31	53	13	6	1	3
37	38	23	11	8	5	4	2
36	26	24	22	21	9	10	
34	28	25	20	15	13	12	
32	30	23	18	16	14	11	

Jumpstart 39
Number Place: 55, 67, 70; 55, 62, 66; 49, 50, 94; 75, 104, 118
Fast Math: 70, 70, 50, 90, 60, 80
Think Tank: 5
Data Place:

Veggie	Tally	Number
Carrots	IIII	4
Peppers	卌 I	6
Potatoes	卌 卌	10

1. potatoes **2.** carrots **3.** 20
Puzzler: 19; 65; 75

Jumpstart 40
Number Place: 41, 33, 28; 59, 49, 39; 83, 38, 33; 117, 105, 99
Fast Math: 69, 50, 70, 44, 77, 60
Think Tank: Answers may vary; check children's drawings.
Data Place:

Monday							
Tuesday							
Wednesday							
Thursday							
Friday							

0 10 20 30 40 50 60

difference between most and least strokes is 30

Puzzler: (Left to right) F, H, F; H, F, H; H, H, F

Jumpstart 41
Number Place: (Left to right) 33, 86; 75, 41; 99, 15

Fast Math: 32, 53, 58, 34, 12, 49
Think Tank: Answers may vary; sample answer: 3 dimes, 2 nickels, 1 penny
Data Place:

Books Read	Tally	Number of People
0	II	2
1	卌 I	6
2	卌 IIII	9
3	卌	5

1. 2 **2.** 6 **3.** 2
Puzzler: 1. 71 **2.** 97 **3.** 15 **4.** 24

Jumpstart 42
Number Place: (Left to right) 39, 28, 43; 64, 17, 52; 46, 100, 71
Fast Math: 33, 34, 40, 51, 75, 22
Think Tank: 6
Data Place: 1. ring toss **2.** face painting **3.** 3 **4.** 9
Puzzler:

Jumpstart 43
Number Place: (Left to right) <, >, <; >, >, <
Fast Math: 41, 98, 50, 78, 89, 22
Think Tank: 30
Data Place:

Class	Girls	Boys	Total
1A	**13**	14	27
1B	14	14	**28**
1C	14	**3**	27

1. 1B **2.** 1A **3.** 27 students
Puzzler: (Top to bottom) I, U, O; O, A, E

Jumpstart 44
Number Place: less than 20—0, 8, 12, 17; between 21 and 50—26, 31, 39, 40, 48; greater than 50—63, 77, 81, 86, 89, 95
Fast Math: 31, 60, 89, 21, 90, 30
Think Tank: 9
Data Place: jeans only—Ben, Dawn, Henry; glasses only—Ann, Carl, Gina; both—Ella, Fritz
Puzzler: 8, 16, 9

Jumpstart 45
Number Place: (Top to bottom) 7, 2; 8, 9; 2, 4; 9, 0; 6, 3; 3, 1
Fast Math: 60, 20, 80; 30, 50, 80; 40, 40, 80
Think Tank: 7
Data Place:

Child	Letters in First Name	Letters in Last Name	Total Number of Letters
Vara	9	11	20
Anna	9	12	21
Tala	10	9	19

1. Tala **2.** Anna **3.** Anna

Answers

Puzzler: Both lines are the same length, but the arrows make one look longer than the other.

Jumpstart 46
Number Place: (Left to right) 74, 45, 81; 67, 98, 56; 25, 82, 57; 4, 33, 48
Fast Math: 60, 30, 30; 80, 50, 30; 90, 60, 30
Think Tank: 15
Data Place: 1. jungle gym **2.** seesaw **3.** swing **4.** 16
Puzzler: 1. stapler **2.** chair **3.** boot **4.** bus

Jumpstart 47
Number Place: Answers will vary; check for accuracy.
Fast Math: (Left to right) 4 + 7 = 47; 12 − 6 = 18; 20 − 10 = 30
Think Tank: Check children's drawings; fourths means having 4 equal pieces.
Data Place:

Letter	Tally	Number
a	I	1
b	I	1
d	IIII	4
e	IIII	4
f	II	2
r	II	2
t	I	1

Puzzler: 1. pitcher **2.** bathtub **3.** bucket **4.** teapot

Jumpstart 48
Number Place: 78, 79, 80, 81; 50, 51, 52, 53; 99, 100, 101, 102
Fast Math: (Left to right) 14, 10, 8; 10, 5, 22
Think Tank: 10 + 0, 9 + 1, 8 + 2, 7 + 3, 6 + 4, 5 + 5
Data Place: 1. Tuesday, January 27 **2.** 5 **3.** 44 inches **4.** less
Puzzler: 1. equal **2.** hundred **3.** number **4.** quarter **5.** twenty **6.** zero

Jumpstart 49
Number Place: Check that children correctly numbered 97 through 108, except 101.
Fast Math: Check children's shadings.
Think Tank: rectangular prism; pyramid; cube
Data Place: Answers may vary; check for reasonableness; because the measuring tools are different sizes
Puzzler: 1, 5, 6, 9

Jumpstart 50
Number Place: 7, 8; 9, 0
Fast Math: $\frac{1}{4}, \frac{1}{2}, \frac{1}{4}, \frac{1}{2}$
Think Tank: 5
Data Place: 1. lemonade **2.** ice cream **3.** watermelon **4.** 15
Puzzler: Check children's problems and answers.

112